ADVENTURE NANNIES

Tales of Wonder,
Wildness, and Wisdom

Compiled by Shenandoah Davis

Adventure Nannies Copyright © 2025 by Shenandoah Davis.

All rights reserved. No part of this publication may be reproduced, distributed or transmitted in any form or by any means, including photocopying, recording, or other electronic or mechanical methods, without the prior written permission of the publisher, except in the case of brief quotations embodied in critical reviews and certain other noncommercial uses permitted by copyright law.

Although the authors and publisher have made every effort to ensure that the information in this book was correct at press time, the authors and publisher do not assume and hereby disclaim any liability to any party for any loss, damage, or disruption caused by errors or omissions, whether such errors or omissions result from negligence, accident, or any other cause.

Disclaimer: This book is designed to provide general information for our readers. It is sold with the understanding that the publisher is not engaged to render any type of legal, business or any other kind of professional advice. The content of this book is the sole expression and opinion of each author, and not necessarily that of the publisher. No warranties or guarantees are expressed or implied by the authors' choice to include any of the content in this volume. Neither the publisher nor the authors shall be liable for any physical, psychological, emotional, financial, or commercial damages, including, but not limited to, special, incidental, consequential or other damages. The reader is responsible for their own choices, actions, and results.

Published by Prominence Publishing.

ISBN: 978-1-990830-90-7

Table of Contents

Introduction
    By Shenandoah Davis 1

Chapter 1: From Wanderlust to Enterprise –
The Adventure Nannies Origin Story
    By Brandy Schultz 7

Chapter 2: It's Not a Job, It's a Lifestyle
    By Meaghan Tyrrell 17

Chapter 3: Becoming Nanny Jess
    By Jess Dickerson 27

Chapter 4: The Festival, The Commune, and The Musician
    By Sam Huntley 37

Chapter 5: The Modern Nanny: From Burnout to Boundaries
    by Sarah Carlisle Stewart 49

Chapter 6: My Journey to Living the American Dream
    By Kim K. Morgan Smart 59

Chapter 7: More Than "Just a Nanny"
    By Emma Hughes 77

Chapter 8: Adventure is a Mindset
    By James Austin V 89

Chapter 9: Mom Boss Magic
    By Reagan Fulton 97

Conclusion
    By Shenandoah Davis 109

Introduction

By Shenandoah Davis

Whenever someone first hears the name of our business, their mind either jumps immediately to women free-climbing cliff faces with babies in Moby wraps, to Mary Poppins flying off into the sky with her flower-brimmed hat and black umbrella, or the most recent salacious news article about celebrities and former nannies accusing each other of poor behavior. Some folks will share that they were a babysitter in their tweens, while others will share that they had an au pair who lived with them for a year or two when their kids were younger. After they've shared their immediate reactions, they usually say, "Does Adventure Nannies do something like that?"

Well…sort of, and also sort of not at all.

What started out over twenty years ago with one enterprising young Coloradoan branding herself as "The Adventure Nanny" has turned into one of the largest recruitment firms for nannies, private educators, and newborn care specialists in the United States. We've spoken at childcare, entrepreneurial, and industry conferences and events all over the U.S. and U.K. We've worked with thousands of families from various industries, backgrounds, and income levels across the country. We've developed decades-long relationships of trust, respect, and candor with nannies, educators, and caregivers. We've been featured and quoted in press outlets like Forbes, the New York Times, Fortune, and many others. But to someone on the outside of Adventure Nannies, the guessing game of what Adventure Nannies actually is, and what we actually do, is often a rough hypothesis or a misguided assumption.

There is no quick elevator pitch to describe the amazing folks we have gotten to know over the years. As you will learn in this book, an Adventure Nanny is not a teenager with a ponytail who goes to someone's house to stare into the glowing screen of their phone all day and hopefully unloads the dishwasher if you remind them, or someone who takes your children to the park to meet up with their friends for a few hours on every sunny day. They are growth-oriented professionals with dynamic, rich backgrounds and lives who, like the families we get to meet, are pursuing life to the fullest and setting their own course for designing their futures.

I had the dream for this book after running an event called Nanny Camp with Reagan Fulton, who you'll meet a little later in this book. Sixty nannies joined us at a summer camp in the Northeast to recharge, spend a few days in the woods, and have rare moments of connection with other nannies (a rare occasion since nannying is often an isolating job without co-workers, or even adults, around for the bulk of the work day.) I thought, over the years, I'd gotten to know many of our candidates fairly well between Zoom interviews, training events, and industry conferences, but there's nothing that brings folks together like a campfire under a starry sky. I got to take a break from being the owner and CEO of Adventure Nannies and connect on a human level with some Adventure Nannies themselves, the heroes of our business and the turning point of many families' success stories, and listen to real stories—not a rehearsed interview response or an AI-created paragraph at the top of a resume. I got to meet teachers who had been burned out on the public education system and who had re-ignited their passion for helping kids learn through running pod schools or acting as homeschooling teachers for touring

INTRODUCTION

bands and on movie sets. I met people who, because of the warmth and support of their employers, came out as LGBTQIA+ at work before they were able to come out to their families or closest friends. I half-joke with the team at Adventure Nannies that our 10-year-goal is to send the first nanny to space, but all kidding aside, we've watched in awe as the nannies we've worked with have gone to the White House, visited over forty countries and counting while working, ascended fourteeners, sailed through the Mediterranean, and homeschooled from an RV visiting every national park in the US. The nannies we've met are heroes in obvious ways, like saving kids' lives in terrifying emergency situations, and heroes in minuscule, nearly-invisible ways, like helping children finish their homework at the dinner table so that their parents can run for public office, follow their own creative or artistic pursuits, run businesses that make the world a better place, and care for other members of their families.

Before we fully dive in and hear from the Adventure Nannies themselves, reading their stories over the past few months has inspired me to share a little bit of my own.

In 2015, I turned 30 and thought I'd had enough adventures for my lifetime—after getting a degree in opera performance, I'd recorded and released a few albums of original songs and played shows in Japan, Australia, all over Europe, and all over the United States. I'd slept on couches, floors, and a porch or two and lugged my seventy-pound keyboard case on trains, planes, ferries, busses, and anywhere else I was invited.

I never thought my musical passion and first career would fade. I got my first toy keyboard at three years old and had studied piano ever since. But I was exhausted by my self-propelled adventures and, for the first time, considered a move to traditional work. Luckily, before I found a cookie-cutter job, Adventure Nannies found me. I knew the founder, Brandy, and her now-husband from my hustling days on tour, and before I knew it, I became a trusted source of advice to her and the small AN team before joining them full-time in 2016 and becoming business partners in 2021.

The leap from artist to nanny agency owner may seem a little unorthodox, but the more I've met other entrepreneurs, the more I've found that few people's paths to their passions are a straight line. It also turns out that DIY musicians have a whole lot in common with nannies. We're resourceful and shrewd when we need to be, we consistently show up even when everyone else around us doesn't, we're historically undervalued and underpaid, and the work we do is driven by a passion so deep that even we can't escape it.

Art and music enrich peoples' lives, but childcare makes their lives possible. The United States is in a childcare crisis. Since the COVID-19 pandemic, as many as two million women have left the workforce, with a main reason being cited as a lack of access to affordable childcare. One day, if we have anything to say about it, there will be a world where childcare is valued and prioritized—by families, by our government, and by businesses. Childcare is the key to gender equity for many families in the United States, and there is a future where affordable childcare is considered as crucial a benefit and right as healthcare or access to food. Until that day comes, I'm proud and grateful for how we've been able to support thousands of families through our agency and through our community by providing resources and best practices, setting industry standards, and being prepared to lend a listening ear at any moment, and for every crisis or celebration. It's become one of the greatest honors of my life to be able to holistically support every person in a nanny equation: parents who are feeling stuck and frustrated, constantly having to choose between what is best for their children, their marriages, and themselves without outside support; nannies who are balancing their own families and pursuits for the greater good of supporting these families; and the young, impressionable minds and hearts of the children, who all of us put first at every opportunity.

The nannies who contributed to this book are at the heights of their careers, but it hasn't always been that way for them. As you'll hear in their stories, everyone found nannying through their own path. For some, this has or will become a lifelong career, and for others, nannying is a brief chapter in their life story. Past Adventure Nannies have moved on to lead a former nanny family's non-profit or NGO. Some have pivoted into tech careers or headed to grad school. Many, like some of these authors, have become parents and nanny employers themselves and have now navigated the full spectrum of the village it takes to raise gentle, resilient, secure children.

I became a musician to travel the world, to meet interesting people, and to get access to spaces and communities I never would have even known about. Nearly twenty years later, I'm still exploring and being invited to the most intimate conversations and the deepest confessions and being introduced to resilient, talented, creative people every day. They just happen to be carrying wet wipes instead of instruments these days.

Welcome to *Adventure Nannies*.

Chapter 1

From Wanderlust to Enterprise – The Adventure Nannies Origin Story

By Brandy Schultz

I thrive in chaos. Growing up with three brothers and wildly dysfunctional parents, I took on the role of a mother for my entire family at a young age. I loved my brothers deeply, and I grew fiercely protective of them. But, at the same time, I dreamed of something more than the day-to-day care of others. I daydreamed about travel and making a difference in the world, but I knew that without a plan, there was no way I'd have the means to leave our town, much less make those dreams real.

Then, when I was 14, I caught a break. My older brother and I both got jobs at a local go-kart track. I was thrilled to escape my in-home duties and poured myself into that place, and babysitting gigs, all the way through high school. I watched as friends headed off to college, but somehow, that path never called to me. While they were off racking up student loans, babysitting gigs turned into full-on nanny jobs, and I was quickly making more money than they were—without any of the debt.

Not one to sit still, I spent my early adulthood bouncing from job to job, each experience feeding my need for exploration and independence. I became a kayak guide, earned my certification as a wilderness first responder, worked at a traveling bicycle and beer festival, and was a nanny for families who took me with them on their vacations. Somewhere along the way, I realized that without planning it, I had created a unique life for myself. Without knowing it, Adventure Nannies was born.

The Adventure Nanny

As families began to request me as a travel nanny, I threw myself into the work, making their family adventures as memorable and stress-free as possible. I took care of their kids, but I also infused each day with wonder, encouraging the kids to explore, ask questions, and build lasting memories. Traveling with families became both my main passion and my primary income. I found myself visiting places I had only dreamed of: the beautiful lakes of Wisconsin, the bustling streets of New York City, the winding canals of Paris and Venice, the wilds of Muskoka in Canada, even the desert of Burning Man.

Between trips with families, I lived in a three-bedroom house with eleven people, mostly musicians who traveled as much as I did. I spent my twenties in a dream world of rooftop coffees and magical house shows, acting as a tour manager for friends' bands, nannying for amazing families, and traveling non-stop. My life felt like a magical combination of music, adventure, and community, and every day felt like an opportunity to experience something new. I was, without question, the luckiest person alive.

During those years on the road as a tour manager, I met Shenandoah, a Seattle musician who was a legend in her own right. Shenandoah and I hit it off immediately, sharing a deep appreciation for adventure, independence, and a slightly chaotic love of life. We stayed in touch over the years, and although we were often on different paths, we always seemed to reconnect. When I posted on social media looking for marketing help for Adventure Nannies, Shenandoah responded. What I thought would be a simple partnership soon turned into something much more. Shenandoah's talents went far beyond marketing—she had an incredible knack for organization, strategy, and building efficient processes that could support our growing business.

Together, Shenandoah and I restructured Adventure Nannies. She brought a level of operational excellence I hadn't even realized we were missing. With her help, we developed protocols and processes that allowed us to serve more families and nannies without sacrificing the personal touch that made us unique. We were doing better than ever, and I couldn't have been prouder of how far we had come.

The Birth of Adventure Nannies

As demand for my travel nanny services grew, so did my personal life. I was falling in love. Wes had moved to Denver with his bandmate to save money, and shortly after arriving, they ended up playing at a house party I threw. We started off as friends, but as time went on, I found myself completely captivated by him. Eventually, it became impossible to resist. At the time, The Lumineers were occasionally outnumbering the crowds they played, and I knew I would need to support him for the rest of his life.

By then, I had started referring families I couldn't travel with to friends who were just as dynamic, trustworthy, and adventurous. I knew of no other travel nanny agencies at the time, and I started to wonder if I could turn this into a legitimate business. For my birthday that year, Wes surprised me with a gift that would change everything: he paid his friend in cases of beer to build the first Adventure Nannies website.

I had no idea what it would take to become a business owner. I had no savings, no business degree, and nothing to fall back on. But I had an idea and the determination to see it through. Through countless mistakes, sleepless nights, internet wormholes, and sheer persistence, we went live. The site wasn't flashy, but it was enough to let families know what we offered and to attract the kind of clients who might be open to the idea of "Adventure Nannies."

Around this time in 2012, something unexpected happened: The Lumineers' song "Ho Hey" exploded. What had started as a modest venture to support us both took an unexpected turn as their music career skyrocketed. Overnight, Wes was on the road constantly, playing sold-out shows across multiple time zones. And so, Adventure Nannies took to the road with him. I became adept at juggling work from tour buses, backstage areas, and hotel lobbies, making time zone changes work as best I could. It was hectic, haphazard, and totally chaotic, but we made it work. Each night, as he played to packed venues, I handled emails, coordinated nanny placements, and fielded calls from clients across the country. Adventure Nannies was a business born from an unorthodox lifestyle, so working remotely from the road was just part of the adventure.

Taking a Risk on the First Clients

With the website live, I knew I needed to take a bold approach to attract our first clients. Rather than going the conventional route, I decided to try cold-emailing potential clients directly. Along with my former nanny business partner, we crafted a series of emails to high-profile families—people we felt might see the unique value in what we offered.

We had no inside contacts, no industry connections, just a scrappy strategy of guessing email addresses and hoping for a reply. We sent emails to "wife name @ company name .com," hoping to get the attention of families who would be intrigued by our brand of adventurous, educational childcare.

Then, something incredible happened. One of those emails landed us a response from a family I had only ever heard about in headlines—a founder of Google. I could hardly believe it. This wasn't just any family; they were visionaries who saw the world differently and were looking for someone who could bring a new level of experience to their children's lives. They understood what we were offering: an opportunity to immerse their kids in adventures that would broaden their perspectives and deepen their understanding of the world.

Landing that first high-profile family was a breakthrough. It was the validation we needed, proof that there was a market for this idea, and it marked the moment Adventure Nannies began to transform from a personal project into a real business.

Building a Community of Dreamers

With that initial success, Adventure Nannies quickly began to grow. We weren't just a nanny agency; we were creating a network of adventurous caregivers who could offer something far beyond traditional childcare. Our nannies were mentors, role models, and explorers, each one committed to creating meaningful experiences that would impact children for years to come.

Building and managing this community of incredible individuals was both thrilling and exhausting. I was learning on the fly—navigating the challenges of business ownership, dealing with complex family dynamics, and trying to maintain a sense of personal balance amidst the chaos. There were days I felt completely overwhelmed, but I was surrounded by people who believed in what we were building.

The nannies who joined us were nothing short of inspiring. They weren't just looking for jobs; they were looking for purpose. They were teachers, artists, athletes, and musicians, each bringing a unique set of skills and a sense of curiosity that made them the perfect fit for Adventure Nannies. Our clients began to recognize that they weren't just hiring nannies; they were inviting extraordinary people into their lives, people who could help shape their children's values and passions.

A New Era With Shenandoah

In 2019, I had my first child, and I knew it was time to step away, at least temporarily, to focus on this new chapter of life. I asked Shenandoah if she would step in as CEO during my maternity leave. Not only did she take on the role with grace, but Adventure Nannies began to flourish under her leadership. Her operational skills and strategic thinking were exactly what we needed to keep growing sustainably, and before long, we were performing better than ever.

It was clear that Shenandoah was the perfect fit for the role, so I made her the permanent CEO. I've never looked back.

A Shared Vision for Adventure

Reflecting on this journey, I realize that Adventure Nannies' success rests on the shoulders of fellow dreamers and adventurers. This business wasn't built by one person; it was built by a community of passionate individuals who saw the value in creating experiences that could change lives. Our first family, our early clients, and the incredible nannies who joined us—they are all part of this story. Each of them saw the beauty in what we were trying to do, and together, we built something that transcended the traditional concept of childcare.

Starting Adventure Nannies was a leap into the unknown. I had no experience, no safety net, only the hope that there were other people out there who believed in the magic of adventure as much as I did. Today, I see our families, nannies, and children as extensions of that original spirit. We're not just offering childcare; we're offering a chance to inspire young minds, to connect families with meaningful experiences, and to support a generation of curious, compassionate, and adventurous people. It's a mission that goes far beyond business—it's a shared dream made real.

In the years since we launched, Adventure Nannies has grown beyond anything I could have imagined. We've now been in business for over a decade, placing hundreds of incredible nannies with families who share our vision. Each placement is a new opportunity to foster creativity, wonder, and connection, a chance to bring a sense of adventure into a child's life.

In many ways, this journey has been a reflection of my own life: a blend of courage, chaos, and community. I've had to learn as I go, relying on the support of people who understand that adventure is more than just a word; it's a way of living, a way of seeing the world, and a way of inspiring others to do the same.

About Brandy Schulz

Brandy Schultz is the founder of Adventure Nannies, a trailblazing agency that connects adventurous families with exceptional nannies, educators, and caregivers. Since its inception, Adventure Nannies has transformed the landscape of childcare by combining education, exploration, and care into a single mission-driven service.

In addition to leading Adventure Nannies, Brandy is the founder of Sound Future, a non-profit organization tackling climate change through creative collaboration and ecological restoration. Her latest initiative, *Surf and Turf*, exemplifies her commitment to sustainability and innovation.

Based in Denver, Brandy spends much of her time on the road, touring with her husband's band, The Lumineers, alongside their two young children. Whether she's brainstorming new projects on the tour bus, tending to her wild plant garden at home, or inspiring others through her ventures, Brandy embodies a life of curiosity, creativity, and purpose.

Chapter 2

It's Not a Job, It's a Lifestyle

By Meaghan Tyrrell

Following my passion for supporting families has evolved into my dream job as a traveling and touring nanny/family assistant. I am a certified Montessori Instructor for children zero to three with twelve years of professional nannying experience and a passion for organization and travel. Nannying has allowed me to live out my strengths and passions daily. Reflecting on my career as a professional in the childcare industry, I can't help but think of how I got here. It all started with my own childhood and upbringing.

My parents got divorced when I was three years old. After years of custody battles, my mom finally got full custody of me and my siblings, losing everything she had in the process. Her parents had both died just before I was born. They left her their family cabin in Wisconsin, which she sold to pay for her divorce lawyers. She used every asset she had to gain custody of us kids. Not only did my mother quite literally give up everything she had for us, but she did it with virtually zero support. I am blown away by my mom's courage and determination. The love and devotion she had for my siblings and me was remarkable.

My mom moved us all to an old farmhouse surrounded by corn fields outside Chicago, Illinois. We would play and wander for hours in the cornfields surrounding our house. My siblings and I were raised like free-range chickens. We did not have very much structure or discipline, but boy, did we have space to roam. My mom worked full time, leaving us kids to fend for ourselves more times than not. My mom tried her best to give us a wonderful childhood. She chose to move us to this old farmhouse because it was all she could afford, but also, it was in a fantastic school district. My mom was raised a catholic and went to an all-girls private school. She wanted that for me and my siblings. Due to her newfound circumstance of raising five kids alone, it wasn't feasible. Instead, her best option was putting us in a public school in a great school district. I thank her for having the foresight to do so. Beyond school, the other structures my mom instilled in us kids were church and sports. We went to church most Sundays, and on Wednesday nights, we did Bible studies. My mom even ran my Bible study group one year. For free-range children, my mom did an excellent job at providing structure and a balanced life for us. That isn't to say we never struggled. We were on food stamps and the free and reduced lunch program at school. I even remember the church helping us get by with gas vouchers and winter coats.

You might be wondering, "What does being raised by a single mother barely keeping it together have to do with my career as a professional nanny/family assistant?" Well, my mom always set clear expectations for us kids: get dressed, brush our teeth, get to the bus stop on time, and complete our assigned chores. She would wake us up in the mornings, then head out the door, not to return until six o'clock at night or later. We all got ready for school alone and returned home from school alone. We always had each other, of course. Aside from her day job as a bookkeeper, she was volunteering at the church, maintaining the old barn house, keeping up on our schooling, taking us to gymnastics and baseball lessons, and putting food on the table every night. There was no doubt my mother worked hard. As a kid, seeing her drive to provide for us made me never want to disappoint her or add more to her plate. So, I made sure to meet her expectations for me and took my little brother under my wing.

My little brother was diagnosed with ADD/ADHD when he was very young. Simple tasks were very challenging for him. He needed someone to keep him on track at all times. When I was in the second grade, and he was in kindergarten, I was getting myself and my brother ready for school every day. It was no small feat getting him dressed and keeping him at the bus stop while we waited for the bus. I found so much joy in helping and protecting my little brother. He was brilliant in his own way. He could take almost anything apart and put it back together, most of the time. There is a saying that goes, "To know a child is to love a child," and that could not have been truer for my brother. My brother taught me true patience and responsibility. This is where my passion for childcare was ignited.

My goal as a childcare provider is to be the support I wish my mom had when raising us kids and to provide consistent, reliable, positive care for children. If my mom had someone she could trust and rely on, she would have been able to enjoy motherhood and relieve some of the stress it undoubtedly brought. Aspects of my upbringing that I apply to my caregiving style today are giving kids loads of time outside without hovering over their every move, letting them get lost in their play, and having them practice problem-solving. I also include them in chores and everyday tasks to teach them responsibility and grow their confidence, giving them purpose and meaning.

In my current position as a travel-touring nanny/family assistant, I have a unique perspective that combines childcare, travel, and adventure in a way that few people get to experience. Imagine living out of a suitcase for weeks, if not months, on end, never staying in one place for more than a few nights. Continuous packing and unpacking, keeping track of every item, day in and day out. For the last seven years, I have not had a typical nanny job but rather a lifestyle that combines caregiving with constant travel. I actually did not know what I was signing up for exactly. I walked into my interview thinking it was a typical nanny position with a travel-loving family. Before my interview, the adventure nannies team asked that I call them when I was five minutes away from the family's home. When I called, I was informed that I would be interviewing with the founder of Adventure Nannies at the time and her famous musician husband, Wesley Schultz of the Lumineers. Having been a fan of The Lumineers' music and knowing I was interviewing for the founder of the agency I was working with naturally elevated my nerves. After the call, I sat in my car down the street from their house. I had given myself plenty of time to get there, so I had a moment to give myself a pep talk. I reminded myself of my beliefs as a nanny to support families in parenthood to the best of my abilities and to be a reliable, trusted ally. I had hopes of making parenthood more enjoyable while being a consistent, dependable, positive figure for children. The challenges of motherhood do not discriminate. It doesn't matter who you are: everyone needs support, and raising kids is not a one-person job.

As soon as I walked in, Brandy and Wes relieved any nerves I had. My boss mom, Brandy, was a former nanny. She naturally has a very warm, welcoming, honest personality. It felt almost as if I was walking into my sister's home or as if we had already known each other for years. I gave them so much credit and grace for welcoming a stranger into their home during this precious time. Lenny, their firstborn, took my breath away at first sight. He was five weeks premature and the smallest baby I had ever seen. We sat in their kitchen, circling the kitchen island on a cold February day. Looking into Brandy's sleep-deprived, drained, new mother's eyes made me want to go into full nanny mode right then and there. In the first months after birth, while the new baby needs love and care, the new mom desperately needs it too. We talked about what they were looking for in a nanny and where they needed help. The interview ended with me starting a trial week the following week. I did what I do best and simply made myself of service, focusing on meeting Brandy's needs so she could enjoy and soak up this precious time with her new baby. Lenny was twenty days old at this time; he will be turning seven years old in just a few months.

My position has evolved and flourished in more ways than I could have imagined over the years. The Schultz family and I have navigated touring the world together, welcoming a new baby and the transition from one to two kids, health troubles, the passing of pets and family members, adding, training, and letting go of new employees, starting a new company, and moving and buying homes. This has taken much patience and grace from all parties. I am so proud of all we have accomplished and overcome over the years.

I remember when I found out Wes was releasing a new album. It was incredibly exciting, but it also meant the scope of my job was shifting. Up until that point, we had only traveled nationally. We had made family trips to their property in upstate New York staying in yurts, family vacations to California, and road trips around Colorado. The travels to come would be on a much grander scale, as you could imagine. World tours with a baby are quite the adventure. We have since circled the globe with both kids in tow multiple times. Some of my favorite places were Australia, Japan, South Africa, Ireland, and The Bahamas.

Behind the scenes, a traveling tour nanny has its glamorous parts. I have more experiences under my belt than I could have dreamed of, from staying in world-class five-star hotels and enough stories to last me a lifetime. Most of my family have never even traveled internationally. The first time I flew on an airplane, I was nineteen years old, visiting home from my live-in nannying job in Portland, Oregon. I am now on my third passport and have been to more cities and countries than I can count.

One of my wildest experiences was flying in a helicopter over the cliffs of Moher in Ireland with the Schultz family. The helicopter had a total engine failure just as we cleared a mountain range, resulting in us free falling out of the sky while the helicopter cab filled with smoke. Miraculously, we landed aggressively but safely in a field full of sheep. Lenny was 20 months old, but somehow, he stayed fast asleep in his father's arms during the entire ordeal. The Schultz family and I have also been lost with no cell signal in Italy, resulting in us hiking through brush and running on a narrow highway with a double stroller. Taking turns to be the leader running at the front of the group, braving the oncoming cars zooming past us. Another memorable experience was taking turns free diving in the Bahamas, spearing lobster that we would eat for dinner that evening while caring for the kids as they napped, snacked, and played, in between taking them for swim breaks in the middle of the ocean. This just scratches the surface of the wild adventures we have experienced together.

Being a travel nanny allows you to impact children's lives in a way that transcends ordinary caregiving. You're not just providing them with day-to-day care but introducing them to the wider world, guiding them through formative experiences, and giving them a sense of stability in the midst of constant change. Of all the amazing experiences this position has brought me, the best part of my job is the bond that I have formed with the kids over the years. My relationship with them is something that I will cherish forever.

My goal remains the same on and off the road: provide stability and support. When you are constantly moving and your external environment is constantly changing, I've found it is crucial to maintain a sense of consistency for the kids where possible. Keeping the kids on the same schedule and routines as we did at home was our saving grace. However, we also needed to be flexible for whatever the day might bring. The kids got accustomed to taking naps on moving tour buses and planes, in random hotel rooms, in green rooms backstage, or in strollers walking around a random city waiting for the hotel room to be ready. I manage to maintain consistency by doing all the same things we would at home: diaper change, sleep sack, bottle, read a familiar book, sing the same song, and place them in their pack and play or bunk with the same lovey or blanket. By giving them all the same sleep signal cues with a great deal of patience and practice, both kids have become amazing travelers. Kids, in general, are resilient, but it has been incredible watching their ability to adapt to new locations, cultures, and time zones.

Things like jet lag, homesickness, and the exhaustion that comes with being "on" all the time are just some of the challenges. Tour dates also tend to land over holidays. There have been many times that I have missed holidays and family events, but that is simply the nature of the job. Maintaining healthy relationships outside of work can be challenging when you are gone for months at a time or leaving at a moment's notice. The thrill of new destinations, a flexible mindset, and gratitude have allowed me to push through these challenges.

I am beyond grateful for the experiences and incredible people caregiving has brought into my life. The joy of supporting children and watching them grow and meet milestones is priceless. Nannying has allowed me to reach my personal goal of purchasing my own home and investing in my loved ones. Nannying and caregiving has been a wildly fulfilling career. I am proud to be a nanny.

About Meaghan Tyrrell

Meaghan Tyrrell is a seasoned travel tour nanny and family assistant with a wealth of experience, having toured the world for the past seven years. Originally from Chicago, IL, Meaghan now calls Colorado home when she's not on the road. With 12 years of professional caregiving expertise, she brings an exceptional level of dedication and skill to each family she supports. Meaghan is a certified Montessori instructor for children aged zero to three, focusing on nurturing independence and fostering a love for learning from an early age.

Meaghan's work is rooted in her core values: family, outdoor exploration, health, and organization. Her passion for the outdoors and commitment to wellness shine through in her caregiving approach, often incorporating active, nature-based experiences into her routines with children. Known for her calm presence and exceptional organizational skills, Meaghan is adept at maintaining a well-balanced environment, even in the fast-paced world of travel. For Meaghan, caregiving is not just a profession but a way to help families create meaningful memories, no matter where in the world they are.

Chapter 3

Becoming Nanny Jess

By Jess Dickerson

As a kid, I found joy in babysitting and earning small rewards for caring for the kids in my neighborhood as soon as I was old enough. This love for nurturing continued into college, where I nannied for a large and dynamic Italian-American family, feeling like I had discovered a perfect blend of work and play. After graduating with a degree in Spanish and International Business with International Affairs, I set off to Mexico with hopes of pursuing international trade, but life led me to roles in education, social work, and crisis counseling instead. Still, I nannied for my very first infant in Mexico. It felt like an answer to prayer. It was part-time, but the introduction to postpartum and newborn care was the most fulfilling role I held. The infant's grandmother was quite involved and became my mentor in a way. I don't think either of us knew the extent to which her wisdom would be the foundation of my career years later, but it was certainly transformative.

In 2015, after a decade abroad, I returned to my roots in Florida for a moment, then began a 17-month journey of couchsurfing across the US, Canada, Mexico, and China, embracing diverse cultures and reinventing myself in queer spaces I encountered along the way. This style of travel allowed me to stay with local hosts in their homes, be part of their everyday lives, and offer my support as a temporary member of their village. I stayed with all kinds of hosts and in some of the most unique and diverse living situations. I found myself observing the varying family dynamics of my host families as I would respectfully fold myself into the daily lives and traditions of old friends, new friends, and strangers who would become friends, much like I had learned to do in my years in Mexico. These couchsurfing opportunities became experiences that would prepare me for travel roles, live-in nanny roles, and doula roles later in my career.

I also sharpened my skills in crisis counseling when I took on jobs in domestic violence and later on a national crisis texting hotline, where I offered empathy and support during times of overwhelming need, especially during the height of the pandemic. After years of this work and supporting my own village through the global crisis, I was facing burnout. I knew I needed to pause and focus on my own healing. It was during this time of reflection that I rediscovered the joy of creating—painting, macrame, digital art, and songwriting became my sanctuary. As I continued to adjust my focus in my life, I spent more time with my niblings and the other children around me. I found inspiration in their pure light and wonder, reminding me of the nurturing joy I had always possessed. This period of creativity and self-care helped me heal, and I embraced the beauty of reinventing myself, leaning into my creative spirit and the deep desire to nurture that had always been at the heart of my journey.

My goal in this season of life, after crisis work burnout, was to focus on joy and healing. I thought back to the times I felt most joyful at a job. I recalled the fun times with my nanny family through college, and I kept returning to the experience of the newborn in Mexico—the answer to prayer.

The child's parents split up partway through the pregnancy. A first-time mother in her mid-20s was facing parenthood alone. *Abuela*, the mother of the absent parent, stepped in to tend to some of the new mom's prenatal needs. I was among the extended support system she worked to set in place before the baby arrived. I was notified when she went into the hospital, and I was present on the baby's very first day home. I remember walking into their house to find the new mother curled up against the headboard, holding a sleeping baby in the dark, and crying with overwhelm. She didn't even know what kind of help to ask for and seemed to just want to sit in the dark and cry.

Understanding her desire to regulate, I asked if I could start washing the dishes in the sink. With her blessing, I got to work on household chores. The movement in the house seemed to help her feel less alone. Soon, the child's grandmother arrived, and she knew exactly what to do. Working alongside his grandmother over the coming days and weeks taught me so much. She taught us both the gentle and tender ways of holding a newborn, wrapping his "taquito" swaddle, drawing his first baths, how to hold him so he felt secure in the water, supporting the mother's attempts at breastfeeding, and ultimately empowering her when she felt it best to switch to bottle feeding. I even learned how to tie the hammock, which is common in most Mexican bedrooms, to swing a baby to sleep safely. I was with him through his first three years of life. I helped at home until she found the nursery where he'd start at six months, and I was still in the rotation of caregivers to pick him up after that. When I left, he could understand English and Spanish and spoke some of his favorite words in both languages. These sweet memories were vivid at this pivotal time in my life when I was choosing a new direction. I thought, "If I prayed for that child, I can do it again."

I returned to my work with children with a family that had a 5-year-old and a 15-month-old that needed temporary support. It wasn't a newborn, but it was a baby, so I accepted the position. The little one was already on a solid feeding and sleeping schedule, so jumping in with the family felt seamless. On my first day on the job, the five-year-old told me his mom was pregnant! The mother chuckled, then looked at me and said, "We weren't going to tell anyone just yet, but now you know." I was excited. The family kept me coming back on an as-needed basis for family assisting help to get the house ready for baby number three. Again, I was able to be there for the transitional period of welcoming a new baby to the home.

My next full-time family was a family with three children, the youngest being three months, with two-year-old and seven-year-old siblings. The littlest thrived in my care, taught me so much, and affirmed this was the path to joy and healing I was searching for.

I met my next infant, who was five weeks old, the following year. I got to be with him until he was 10 months old. This family was special to me because they were the first parents to ask my pronouns, push through the learning curve, and use they/them successfully. This came as a huge relief because I was working a second nanny job at the time for a family that had one step-parent who was vocally disapproving of LGBTQIA+ culture. My job was simply to pick up two tweenager siblings from school on Friday and drive them an hour and a half across town to the other parent's house as part of a developing parenting plan. I would do the reverse on Monday morning to get them back to school.

To put my situation as a queer person into perspective, this was at the height of the workings of Florida's "Don't Say Gay" bill, which now restricts discussions of sexual orientation and gender identity in certain grades of public schools. While I was not working in a school and could not legally be held to the marginalizing and oppressive limitations of the bill, local supporters of the bill around me were aggressively vocal. Supporters, like the step-parent in reference, considered any childhood exposure to queer culture to be "grooming," even in contexts such as representations of different family structures in storybooks or respecting names or pronouns different from the ones assigned at birth. I found myself shrinking in authenticity as I worked for this family.

Eventually, the oldest started High School and came out to me and their affirming side of the family. Then, they bravely came out at school. In our long drives, they opened up about the unbearable pressure they felt from the other side of their family. My time with that family was coming to an end soon, and I felt the best thing I could do would be to advocate for the teen to start with a counselor or therapist, and they did. While that job was one of the most stifling work experiences for me, I know from my time in crisis work that "just one accepting adult can reduce the likelihood of an LGBTQ young person attempting suicide by 40%."[1]

Continuing my career, I was eager to grow as an infant nanny. I attended my local International Nanny Training Day. During Q&A, I stood up to share my big vision, "As you may already know, Rhianna is pregnant with her second child. If I wanted to apply to be her nanny, what would I have to do?" My question was perhaps whimsical but very serious. I was given

---

[1] The Trevor Project 2022:
https://x.com/TrevorProject/status/1603895504164765696

The Trevor Project [@TrevorProject]. (2022, December 17). Every LGBTQ young person deserves to feel accepted and loved. That's why we're here 24/7, during the holidays and… [Tweet]. X.
https://x.com/TrevorProject/status/1603895504164765696

some guidance on how to get to an International Nanny Association conference. Coincidentally, there was one happening in a few weeks just an hour and a half from my home. With Riri as my guiding star, I showed up on the first day and was amazed by the scale of the event. I couldn't believe I had been so out of the loop and missed out on so many incredible nanny resources and training sessions! Legal pay, what? Nanny contracts, huh? What always seemed like an informal fall-back plan was now taking shape as a formal career path.

So, I polished up my resume, collected reference letters, and dove into training that piqued my interest. I first started with the Newborn Care Specialist training, where I learned the clinical and practical ins and outs of those precious first few weeks of life for the newborn. However, thinking back to my experience with expectant and new parents, I really found joy in supporting them as well. Being present to help with household tasks, support older siblings, and tend to the unique needs of the birthing parent felt like something I wanted to participate in. So, I enrolled in a Full Spectrum Doula course to further that study. During all my studies, I completed the extensive tasks to land a spot on the rosters of highly respected nanny referral agencies I networked with and started applying. I was also responding to jobs on other job boards, looking for the right fit. I had a trial with a local family, and here's how it went...

I connected with the occupational therapist who was in-house that day on ways the practice in OT could be continued day-to-day. My mastery of the Spanish language came in clutch when other household staff arrived without their English-speaking counterpart, and I was able to translate for her and the parents on some essential details. The littlest kiddo shouted to their mom while I pushed them on the swing, "I love Jess! Can Jess come play every day?" While getting the kids set up with dinner, I managed to inspire unique behavior in the cat that had the mother convinced we had some mystical connection. The oldest was tired after a long day of school and did not want to join his father for batting practice in the backyard, yet my enthusiastic curiosity about his baseball skills inspired him to jump up from the couch, grab my hand, and lead me out to the batting cages to show me what he can do. I received a vendor and connected him to the correct point person. I left a clean and tidy play area. When I said goodbye, the oldest asked his mom when I would be back. I was confident I had landed the job. After days of not hearing about the position, I called the referral specialist to get the scoop. She said the father commented that my "style was a bit too funky for his high-profile job." I was crushed. I could hear the queer-phobia in that sentiment, and I felt betrayed by my authenticity.

Fast forward a few interviews later, hair and clothing styled exactly the same as on that failed trial, and I landed my first formal (travel!) contract. This time through Adventure Nannies, the referral agency I met at the INA Conference that could see me in all my funky queerness and tender nanny nurture and seemed eager to back me up. Nothing compares to the feeling of having a standout agency like Adventure Nannies believe in me.

As I drove the 15-hour commute to my first day of a two-month contract, I listened to several AN podcasts to get in the zone. One of my faves was an episode with a non-binary Newborn Care Specialist who talked about their experience as a queer person in the field. I envied their openness on the job and how they leaned on their authentic self-expression to attract aligned clients. I had decided I would have the awkward conversation with my new employers on my first day about my they/them pronouns and hope for the best. I arrived just in time to meet eight-month-old baby E before she went down for bed. She was pure joy, and I had a feeling this would be a cozy, cuddly winter contract. Soon, we sat down for a lovely welcome dinner when something unexpected happened. The mother turned to her music biz husband and said, "Honey, you should ask Jess about their music. I believe I saw in their resume that they sing and play some instruments." Now, that unsolicited use of they/them pronouns was pure music to my ears. Do you know what happened after that? Nothing awkward. Just beautiful dinner conversation flowing and lots of music.

By the end of my contract, Baby E was ten months old and DJing like a pro on her playpad, and I had written lyrics to some of the beats she was spinning. I have a tradition of making art collaborations with all of my kiddos, even the newest of newborns, and presenting them to the parents before my last day. Sometimes, it's visual art, but this time, we made sweet music. I played a track I mixed with audio clips of baby E hitting the button to her favorite beat, the one she knew I would sing along to. I layered her coos and added my vocals. It became a 30-second masterpiece that had dad sobbing in his chair when he heard it. He said I woke something up in her that he recognized as beautiful. Then I got out my ukulele for our encore performance of "The Bottle Song," a comical account of what happens when, as the lyrics begin, "The milk is getting warm, and the baby's getting hungry." Baby E clapped along as she bounced on mom's knee while I sang, and it was evident in our performance that she knew it was her song. I'd say that the contract ended on a high note. It shouldn't be surprising that a referral agency would respect my identity in candid conversations about candidates before hiring, but I was genuinely shocked that I didn't have to go to bat for myself.

My next contract was through Triangle Nannies, another agency I met at the INA conference. I had a similar affirming experience and the joy of being hired on with a queer family. This time, the family took pride in being a safe space for me. In this particular dual-mom household with children assigned female at birth, everyone in the kids' lives, even uncles and the dads of friends at school, were referred to with she/her pronouns at this developmental stage of language. When the toddler twins began speaking in full sentences, I will never forget how their parents handled it. One toddler was sitting on her mother's knee and watched me put on my hat. "Jess put on her hat!" she said. Mom took some hats out of the hat bin a modeled one, "Mama put on her hat. Jess put on their hat." The kiddo repeated and pointed to the people with their hats. Then, pointing to the stuffed toy nearby, Mama said, " Elmo forgot his hat." She received the teaching moment like all the other teaching moments in toddler life then skipped off. Mama thanked me for being down for that little lesson. We found it's really not complicated when children are soaking up all kinds of language anyway. It's less about language and more about the natural unfolding of life. On and on it continues where my skills are aligned with the job and my presence among the family is valued. I am optimistic about my journey ahead as I remain true to myself and open to the next adventure!

About Jess Dickerson

Jess D (they/them) is an Infant and Travel Nanny with training as a Full Spectrum Doula. They have extensive experience in education and supporting people through crisis. Jess is also an artist who loves inspiring the people in their community to nurture their own creative outlets. It's common to find them catching creative inspiration for art while working with families. Their creative outlets include macrame, painting, drawing, songwriting, and playing folk instruments. It is well known among their families that Jess finds joy in the family-assisting duties of being an in-home caregiver. They strive to balance the load on parents so parents can then be more available to contribute to society in other roles that bring fulfillment and keep the household going. In their free time, Jess D is probably singing to the wildlife outside, doing life with their beautiful constellation of chosen family, or dreaming up another art project.

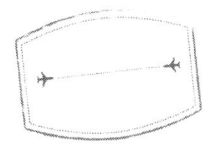

Chapter 4

The Festival, The Commune, and The Musician

By Sam Huntley

"Cool underwear," my nanny kid, let's call her Twinkle, says to me as I pull down my pants to pee in an outhouse. We are at a remote coastal commune in a lush Central American country. Her comment throws me off a little, but I stifle my laughter and say, "Thank you." She is three years old and, like many toddlers, is eager to make observations and share them. We—the parents and I—regularly use a mantra with her, "*gentle, loving-kindness,*" and she is often bursting with the chance to compliment people.

Unknowingly, I was living in a surreal pre-pandemic time. After a few happy years living and working in Los Angeles, I was ready for a different pace of life. I met a new family who offered me a dream role: the chance to travel the world with them while being based in an extraordinary, once-in-a-lifetime location. I broke my lease and quickly moved north to their stunning remote coastal California town. Alas, much of our initial travels were postponed, but five months into the job. It was February of 2020 when we finally embarked on our first (and last) international trip. We were visiting a Central American country for a music festival. It's sweaty, buggy, and full of people who aspire to have a mystical journey in the jungle. It was my second time in this country—my first was after college when I was on a solo journey. As a geeked and eager-to-please nanny, I was honed in on building my career chops and fulfilling my desire to evolve into a travel nanny. My Spanish wasn't perfect, but I quickly proved to be the most confident and willing-to-try speaker in our group. Feeling proud, I took a quick bathroom mirror selfie at a roadside taco stand, giving myself an internal pat on the back.

After a long and bumpy ride from the city to the coast, we arrived at the festival grounds. We knew we would be there for at least one whole week. After that, it was a complete mystery to me and the parents as well—they are the spontaneous type. We hauled our bags to the main gate and finally located the VIP cabanas after some running around. As I caught my breath and adjusted to the tropical climate, I began to realize there wasn't a proper bed for me. This trip was planned with me in mind, but it appeared that this detail had slipped through the cracks. My heart sank a bit. I let them know that I was disappointed by the basic oversight, but I decided to take a solution-oriented approach. I tried to sleep in my camping hammock (that I did think to bring) but ended up sleeping on a makeshift pallet couch under their platformed room and using Twinkle's carrying wrap as my blanket. I was severely lacking a bug net, and I woke up the next morning covered in irritating mosquito bites. I've camped with this family before and countless times on my own, but the planning, or lack thereof, had left me feeling wildly unprepared

The next evening, I was relaxing in my hammock while we were all chatting. Twinkle was running around naked and climbed up to swing with me. I hopped out of the hammock to rock her for a bit when their friend pointed out some mud on my leg. Upon wafting smells and a moment of closer inspection, we collectively realized it was not mud. Twinkle had pooped the hammock. We laughed it off, and I went to locate the showers—which the festival had, thank goodness! This occurred before the weekend part of the festival was underway, when lack of water and long shower lines would become an issue. Though sadly, my hammock was rendered a less desirable sleep spot after the poop incident!

A few nights into the festival, I walked into the bathroom area to get ready for bed. It was abuzz with the chatter and activity of guys and gals readying to dance until sunrise. People were adorned in glitter, neon, and intricately knotted bits of fabric that covered just enough to either hide or reveal intimate body parts. I was the odd one out, readying for a night of sleep. A girl asked me to borrow some toothpaste, which I happily shared. She began to moan and sway while brushing her teeth. Holding back my giggles, I wondered if we were using toothpaste from the same tube. I slunk back to my temporary bunk, which was arranged for after I asked for it. They were understanding, considering I would be working long days on this trip. I made it clear that I am better equipped to do my job when provided with a chance for a good night's sleep.

We spent the week at the festival roaming around, looking for stories and adventures. The day-to-day rituals of the festival were different from ones at home but Twinkle was accustomed to the lifestyle and more than happy to amble about and dance with strangers. A random man she charmed gave her a piece of chocolate, and she proudly took it to her parents and asked, "Can I have this? No mushrooms or cannabis." Twinkle was so fun to be with: always curious, giggly, and eager to befriend critters. A little while later, we found a giant six-inch-long grasshopper, and she carried it on her stroller tray for days—even after it died. We joined many festival-goers who gathered every evening on the beach at sunset to howl as the sun dips into the ocean and the night begins. There was a designated kids area with different stations for interaction: a sprawling tree fort, a curated kid-friendly lineup, and workshops. We found ourselves in the kid zone when we wanted some respite from the crowds or needed a moment. One day we join a child-centered cacao ceremony. Twinkle didn't like the bitter taste of the cacao beverage but sipped from her coconut cup every time she was prompted. I admire her persistence in participating. Cooperatively, we tried new things and embraced the magic as Twinkle guided me effortlessly through her galaxy.

Despite my efforts, my sleep remained strained throughout the festival as I balanced working long days and having to move beds every night. Meanwhile, Twinkle could nap anywhere and was oddly experienced at falling asleep to loud booming beats—this seems to be a norm for kids who go to festivals. During one of my breaks, I noticed a tiny baby snoozing on a yoga mat. This oblivious child was in a deep sleep amidst a crowded tent of perspiring adults, clad in various states of linen and harem. They stretched intensely to thumping eastern-influenced tones while the baby remained as motionless as a dead sea turtle I saw at the beach. Later that day, I was clearing my plate to the compost tent when two people nearby took it from my hands, saying, "We'll take care of that for you." They begin licking my plate fervently and shoving my food scraps into their mouths. I walked away, feeling bewildered and amused, realizing that in this bizarre world, kids aren't the only ones with an uncanny knack for adapting to the oddities around them.

One evening, the parents decided to keep Twinkle up late so we could all go together to see a DJ perform with fire dancers, fire blasters, and lasers all over a tiki-style bamboo stage. Twinkle's young brain was stunned by the display. She danced passionately and squealed with delight at the big fire. I was equally enamored. It reminded me of the 2002 scooby-doo movie. I felt as if the soul-stealing monsters would emerge from the jungle at any moment. As the festival came to a close, I felt appreciative. It wasn't my cup of tea, but it allowed me to stay present in my work. I was tired

THE FESTIVAL, THE COMMUNE, AND THE MUSICIAN

of the long days, constant noise, and hoards of people. We recovered from the festival at a nearby resort. I composed myself and gathered my energy, much like the sloths living on the hotel grounds. We stayed in civilization for a few nights on our way to the next stop of the trip: the commune.

My employers made friends with the founder of the festival and decided we must go to the after-party. He hosts this mini-festival at his personal commune—*ahem*—prominently featured on a television series a couple years after we visited. It sounded like a continuation of the festival to me. I was exhausted by the idea but obligated to follow the whims of my employers. The commune was on a part of the Caribbean that is coast inaccessible by road, which means there are two ways in and out: hire a dinghy or hike. Our baggage and lack of machete made the dinghy option better for us. I would not be leaving until it was over– I'd have to hike or swim out if I wanted to try.

We slowly drove cross-country from the Pacific to the Caribbean side and stopped at a national park along the way. Upon arriving at the commune, I found out I would be sharing a room of bunk beds with Twinkle and her parents, aka my employers. Again, not ideal, but I could deal.

The founder immediately grabbed me at the first meal and tried to woo me into the foliage with tree frog lore. I was not mystified by his rainforest-obsessed charm like everyone else, but even so, I played nice and felt the welcoming energy. His whole schtick seemed to be about making food overly spiritual. Their food was grown and cooked on the property, and it was wholly delicious after eating from the same vendors all week at the big festival.

On our second day at the commune, the founder gave a tour of the property to all forty or so attendees. People attending were musicians, hippies, lost souls, trustafarians, wanna-be shamans, poly-curious, and mother-earth-oriented types. Mostly, they were here because they couldn't stand for the festival high to end. He introduced each plant with unbridled enthusiasm while cutting it open with his machete for all to taste. He would often encourage us to shout a particular spiritual word in unison as we learn about the fruits. Much of the fruit was familiar to me since I previously worked on a farm in the region. Nonetheless, I was delighted to try Australian finger limes and miracle fruit. We individually took turns swishing the same miracle fruit seed around in our mouths, eating some lime, and then waiting for the shocking sweetness to take over. When it's my turn, I swish the seed around my mouth after nine total strangers—*when in Rome,* right? Twinkle and I then exited the tour early to try for a nap.

When the nap was over, everyone had come back from the tour covered in an earthy clay substance and giddy with delight. It turns out they all got naked and rubbed mud on each other. I sensed it was a bonding moment, and I felt squarely outside the group. At the same time, I felt relieved that we left—I'm not sure how I would have come out of that one, professionally speaking. The gap between me and other attendees widened as the weekend continued. I was having a wildly different experience being there for Twinkle. Every now and then, there was an interesting conversation or a jam session to join, but more and more people avoided me. I could only partake so much, as I wasn't taking psychedelics or joining any polycules. I felt bonded to my pursuit to curate Twinkle's experience. I wanted her to have the same freedom to explore and find thrills in this weird place.

One day, Twinkle was having a sad moment, wanting to be with her parents—they were in a breathwork workshop on the yoga deck. The workshop was starting, but we walked over to connect for a bit and watch until she felt ready to go off with me. Her parents are intentional about

THE FESTIVAL, THE COMMUNE, AND THE MUSICIAN

attachment parenting, and we work as a team to perpetuate healthy relationships. Upon our arrival to the deck, two people running the workshop approached us in a confrontational way, saying, "What are you doing here? This is not a place for children." They were very stern and unwelcoming. I calmly explained, "Twinkle wants comfort from her parents." They continued to urge our exit with a demanding tone, "You really can't be here! This is going to be very emotional. There will be screaming and sobbing; it's too much for a child to see!" I told them, "I understand," and took Twinkle elsewhere. The interaction left a rotten taste in my mouth. It dawned on me how unwelcome we (children and caregivers) were there. We are meant to stay on the fringes, not integrate into the experience. It's ironic to me that the adults here seem to be seeking their child-like selves through workshops and psychedelics but aren't willing to connect with an actual child.

By the end of the after-festival party, I was more than ready to leave and was looking forward to spending time in parts of the country that aren't expat communes. But of course, my bosses had connected with a musician who agreed to have us come stay at his hand-built bamboo house at the other commune. This other community had a school and was apparently more family-oriented. The family is naturally curious about what it would be like to live there, so we ventured on with the musician.

We drove through the countryside, crammed in the car. The musician was happy to be getting a free ride back home in exchange for having us stay— at least, that's all that he implied. No surprise, his house is smaller than the picture he painted. My employers and Twinkle stayed on a bed on the lower deck, and he offered me to stay in his bed with him or in a bed next to the family. I'm outwardly disgusted at his suggestion to share a bed with him, and my bosses stay silent. Dumbstruck and delirious, I move the spare mattress to the upper deck and stay there.

Once again, we were in a remote location and stuck here for a few days. Twinkle and I hung around the house and property. We chased blue morpho butterflies aimlessly down the rugged road and said 'hi' to cows we passed. Her stroller was put to the ultimate off-road test and was an indispensable tool for us to navigate the remote terrain. I began to look forward to our endless walks as they became an escape for me, and I would constantly look for ways to prolong them. One day we planned to go swimming at a special river spot. We were about to leave when the musician casually mentioned that people swim naked in the river. My stomach drops. I tell them, "Cool, I'll stay back then and not go to the river if you guys want to go," looking toward my employers. The musician is immediately offended by my choice and retorts, "What's the problem? It's just nudity." I'm clear with him, "I love nude swimming, but it's a professional boundary of mine not to swim naked with my bosses." Twinkle's parents seem to grow offended along with the musician and by me making my boundary clear. It's tense, but I trust my instincts and know I won't regret my decision. One of my employers pulls me aside and says, "Look, I understand because I was once a nanny, but like, we're different." I'm saddened by their response, but I agree with them—they are different.

Confronting the river swimming moment shifted everything. Suddenly, they saw me more as a friend than a professional, struggling to accept my need for boundaries. They took my limits personally, not understanding that these parameters actually allowed me to connect more genuinely, appreciating them as individuals without any blurred lines. What I love most about being a nanny is precisely how fluid this work can be. It's rarely straightforward; it's a job that demands creativity and adaptability at every turn.

THE FESTIVAL, THE COMMUNE, AND THE MUSICIAN

After three intense weeks immersed in their world, we were returning to the United States. I was absolved from work for a week to spend my pre-planned reset time in Austin, Texas, with my sister to process and recover. When I reluctantly returned to California, I debated whether to continue with the family after such an eye-opening trip. Then, just a day later, COVID-19 lockdowns began. During these isolating months, my mind often drifted back to sharing the miracle fruit seed—a surreal, almost mythical memory from a time that suddenly felt far away. The intimacy of the trip that seemed so inappropriate now left me wondering when I would ever be physically close to a group of strangers again.

This Central American expedition was a turning point in defining the kind of nanny I aspired to be. I'd long romanticized the idea of being a travel nanny, imagining a life full of new horizons. After journeying with multiple families, I discovered that my true desire for exploration extended far beyond work. A transformative "mini-commune" tour revealed the importance of balancing my professional role with a strong sense of personal boundaries. Working as a nanny is deeply personal to me, yet this experience made me confront a crucial truth: I thrive when I can clearly define my life outside of work. While the lives of the families I support may overlap with my own, ultimately, it is *their* life, not mine. Despite facing these difficult realities on our trip, I decided to stay on with the family for three more months to support them in a big move while navigating the uncertainty of the early pandemic days.

A few months later, I left amicably. Though we'd shared incredible moments, our lives and goals were distinct in ways that mattered. In the end, I walked away grateful for the experience and the lessons unearthed in that wild, exhilarating journey through the jungle. By the end of the year, as the world felt a bit safer, I set out on a sailing trip—this time, just for me. I joined a group of complete strangers to sail through the

Caribbean, where we danced, shared meals, and slept under the stars on the deck. Yes, we even had moments of spontaneous, carefree skinny dipping. The closeness I'd once feared I'd lost had returned, but now in a way that felt entirely right, exactly as I'd hoped for all along.

About Sam Huntley

Sam is a dynamic author and artist whose debut essay offers a compelling glimpse into her extraordinary journey through multiple creative fields. With a degree in studio art, she launched an enriching, decade-long career as a professional nanny, living and working in vibrant cities across the United States. Early jobs in summer camps and outdoor education gave her invaluable skills and a deep-rooted passion for championing adventurous, wild-hearted kids, setting her apart as an enthusiastic advocate for children's curiosity and growth. Sam's warm, empathetic approach to caregiving—infused with the spirited values of her Minnesotan family—has earned her a stellar reputation as both a caregiver and confidante to countless families. In her free time, she fully embraces her artistic nature: sailing with friends, immersing herself in live music, and traveling widely to engage with contemporary art fairs. Now splitting her time between Minneapolis and Nashville as a sought-after rotational nanny; she continues to share glimpses of her projects, creative life, and inspirations on Instagram at @neonpioneer

Chapter 5

The Modern Nanny: From Burnout to Boundaries

by Sarah Carlisle Stewart

"This has to be a scam," I thought while staring at a LinkedIn recruitment message offering a higher hourly wage as a Nanny/Family Assistant than my young and spry 23-year-old self could ever fathom in my current trajectory as a Behavioral Therapist. At this point in my career, I thought the only avenue to upward financial mobility utilizing my Psychology degree would be to pursue a PhD. In preparation for that application process, I was balancing my time with behavioral therapy and as a research assistant for the Berkeley Early Learning Lab at UC Berkeley and for the East Bay Community Recovery Project in Alameda County. This juggle meant a ridiculously extensive amount of time in my car trekking across the expanse of the San Francisco Bay Area. Coincidentally, I read this message while passing time in a sports complex parking lot, as I often did during my many hour-long gaps between in-home therapy sessions. Instead of this grueling grind, could this actually be a fast track to a sustainable career?

The first nanny I ever knew was my Grandma Gladys. She nannied for families throughout the East Bay Area with me as her tag along. From her example, I knew it was a legitimate career worth pursuing, but I had never considered it could be a financially sustainable one for me. With a recent promotion to Parent Consultant, my caseload increased from five families to seven, and while that meant increased responsibility, it didn't equate to much of an increased wage. Considering a commute to one single location with one family was incredibly tempting, and earning higher compensation doing my work privately as a Nanny/Family Assistant was a bit of a no-brainer. I loved my littles, but I was beginning to feel stifled and just out of reach from meaningful impact due to the systems in place. This way, I could be more intentional and hands-on with my caregiving; I could actually put those skills to use as a nanny providing individualized family care.

After several interviews with placement coordinators, a personal assistant, and the parents themselves, my next career chapter began a month later, in July of 2017. I went from supporting struggling working-class families bidding for more services from the county as a Behavioral Therapist and delving into the lives of young adults experiencing their first episode of early psychosis, often homeless and with basic needs unmet, as a Research Assistant, to working in the tech capital of the world: Silicon Valley. I couldn't anticipate the culture shock I would experience from a mere 50-mile hop across the Bay.

This was the land of Stanford University, of Facebook, of Google. Of private schools and country clubs, modern homes built with service entrances, and fully staffed households. Of angel investors and executives, as well as some of the notoriously hardest-working people in the world.

And also of extreme discretion. This wasn't immediately alarming; I was familiar with operating this way. As a Behavioral Therapist and a Research Assistant, there were a multitude of rules to maintain and protect privacy. I was accustomed to HIPAA compliance, with every written record kept safe behind three locks and my notes written in code. If I saw my clients in public, it was my responsibility to allow them to approach me first.

Though this culture of privacy wasn't new to me, the reasons why were. On day one, I was told my discretion was of utmost priority because Silicon Valley thrived on fishing for insider knowledge to stay one step ahead of each other. The schools even had rules for children: avoid talking about what parents did for a living and avoid talking about what private schools you're applying to or accepted in. I was instructed to be extremely mindful of who I spoke with and what I shared at sports practices and carpool drop-off lines. Without directly saying it, I was to operate with blinders on because there was an underlying thought that personal and professional information could be leaked and gained, particularly by the domestic workers in town. One nanny in town sought more hours providing laundry services to another neighborhood family and was abruptly given a stern talking to for fear they'd give away information, even if unintentionally. This would set the scene for my work and provide the fertile soil for the burnout that would ensue when I inevitably had no one to talk to.

I'm an Enneagram 3 Wing 2, meaning in a few words: I'm a high achiever, and I like helping others. I wanted to be dependable, trustworthy, responsible, and on my A game all the time. I jumped in feet first, hit the ground running, and immediately poured my all into caregiving for this family. But very quickly, my job became vampiric, sucking away at my energy. It was a perfect storm: They were overwhelmed, and I was eager to please, creating endless opportunities to go above and beyond and overextend myself. I said yes to nearly everything regardless of whether I wanted to, whether I felt comfortable and confident in doing so, or whether they were typical for my job scope.

Work again this weekend, and the next, and the next, totaling 28 days of the month? Yes. Come in earlier at 10 am to walk the dog and leave at 10 pm after putting the house to sleep? Yes, no problem. Take the untrained, skittish, rare breed dog to the pet store where it will inevitably wiggle out of its harness and run out the automatic sliding doors, so you chase it down the four-lane main street, even hopping in a stranger's car because in no way could you lose this dog lest you lose this job? Yes, absolutely, I can.

Stay behind to be the only adult supervising this 10-year-old's birthday party where a child will inevitably break their arm riding a ripstik and not have any way to contact their parents? Yes, of course.

I was consistently two bad days away from quitting, and there was little effectiveness in my self-care as it felt foreign, indulgent, and selfish. When I did get a random Sunday off, it felt like a cosplay of an entirely different person's weekend. I no longer had personal interests, hobbies, or experiences. Prior to this job, I took ceramics classes and played tennis, but it had been years since I touched some clay or picked up a racquet. I didn't know who I was apart from my caregiving, further deepening the growing co-dependency.

I was fully burnt out but in so deep that I didn't know *how* to say no. It was utterly unsustainable, but my reputation proved I was capable of operating at this extreme caliber. As a yes person, saying no felt wrong, like I was lying because I *could* do those things. I had an internal battle; I don't want to continue setting precedence for this, but is it petty or uncooperative to stop now? Would I appear lazy, obstinate, or incapable?

My care was no longer authentic, and my resentment was growing exponentially as I felt more and more taken advantage of and frustrated. I became easily annoyed and bitter. Compassion fatigue became an identity crisis. I began to question whether I was actually helpful or empathetic or caring. And if I wasn't, who was I, what was I doing here, what had I been doing with my life?

Burnout, for me, was a full-blown John Steinbeck existential crisis.

Ultimately, all of the going above and beyond, the job creep, the urgent answering of every menial call and text, and the guilt about time off didn't prove my dependability, my responsibility, my competence, or my capability. It actually proved that I was willing to drop everything for others, that I was willing to set myself on fire to keep those around me warm, and that I was willing to betray myself. I molded myself into a happiness pump, doing anything to make others happy at my own expense.

I had actually been self-sabotaging from the start. Operating this way was not only a huge disservice to myself but also to those I cared for because I was showing up empty and inauthentic. What good is my empathy if it's covered in resentment, overextension, and unsustainable habits? I had to redefine my empathy so that it extended to and included myself.

Compassion and empathy are like muscles, and caregivers are predisposed to have an athletic build. Muscles need to be exercised but not overstrained. When you overwork a muscle and stretch it beyond its capacity, injury is inevitable, and it will no longer be able to lift the way it was intended. Similarly, when we overstretch our compassion muscles, we grow compassion fatigue and cannot care to our fullest capability.

Caregiving professions can be burnout landmines because there's such an implicit message to please, to be subservient, to put yourself last, and to be likable and amicable. Those who care the most, with the most compassion, are also the most susceptible to compassion fatigue in the same way a professional skydiver is more likely to end up in a skydiving accident, a firefighter is more likely to inhale smoke, or a hospital worker may be more susceptible to infectious disease.

Though there is susceptibility, burnout doesn't have to be an inevitability when we harness our empathy with boundaries rooted in our self-worth. In nature, bitterness indicates that something is potentially dangerous. Similarly, my bitterness served a function in revealing my boundaries and values. I recognized that saying no to what doesn't serve me was actually the biggest yes, transforming my fears into my freedoms. My boundaries allow me to remain whole and sustainable in my caregiving and to truly be authentically compassionate. Showing that I know what I can do and what I can do *well* proves real competency and capability. A good, helpful, and compassionate domestic worker knows when and how to say no. A good nanny is one who can set boundaries and advocate for their needs.

On the journey to healing my burnout: Boundaries, check. Next comes community.

The Silicon Valley instruction to avoid gossip made a further silo for my burnout to fester. My intentions weren't to gossip about the family's inner secrets. I wanted to ask someone, "Is this normal? Am I going crazy? Am I the only one experiencing this?" In this industry, we don't have stereotypical caregivers, someone we can throw a Jim from The Office side eye to when things get inevitably messy.

Three years into this position, on February 23, 2020, The Modern Nanny was created.

I initially created the Instagram account to combat my own isolation. Despite there being hundreds of thousands of domestic workers here in the US and worldwide, the nature of our job can leave us feeling alone through the sticky icky. Around this time, Instagram launched reels, creating an opportunity to bring joy and humor back into my work, as well as help nannies be seen as whole human beings, not just our caregiving selves. Little did I know that we were on the precipice of a worldwide pandemic, during which we would all need a little online community.

By December of 2020, my Instagram account grew to 2,500 followers with viral reels at 10K views, then 40K, then 100K, and the highest hitting 3 million views. By July of 2021, The Modern Nanny account had grown to 10.1K followers. This rapid growth proved to me that not only was I not alone in my burnout or in my isolation, but the industry needed visibility. We're largely an invisible labor force, and we want to be seen.

On September 30, 2021, my husband and I moved 500 miles south to sunny San Diego, CA. I was heavily involved with the academics of my previous family and was incredibly thankful for the opportunity to continue assisting them remotely in this process, but it was definitely going to look different. I thought this would be the end of my nannying career as I had grown to know it, but this was just another chapter of The Modern Nanny.

Year 1 of The Modern Nanny was making our presence known, making our seat at the table of the industry, and fostering the community.

Year 2 of The Modern Nanny was all about information and education to bring about true advocacy.

Remarkably, I was able to use my rusty research skills, something I thought I had long said goodbye to, to create the Nanny Census in April of 2022. For years, nannies and families would use information from the International Nanny Association's Wage and Benefits Survey to determine what a reasonable market rate was, but there had been a lull in this data collection for 2 years. There was another need for the industry, and I knew I had the skill set to fill it. The Nanny Census would go beyond "What does the average nanny make?" and explore the industry even deeper by asking about wages and benefits, education and experience, retention and satisfaction, and how they all interact with each other. Our first Nanny Census received 670 responses, a small subset but a great start for simply gaining participants from Instagram and Facebook. By our third rollout in January of 2024, we received 2,151 responses rivaling the data sets provided by larger corporations putting out wage information.

Just like I never knew someone could actually make a fruitful, highly compensated career out of nannying, I never considered I could continue in the industry, mentoring and educating others. Now, I'm a childhood caregiver gone child caregiver coach, bringing community to a traditionally coworker-less career with education, humor, and cultural commentary.

It wasn't until I was up on stage at 2024's International Nanny Training Day in San Diego, CA, that I made a grander realization about my divine connection to this industry. Because San Diego, CA, was, in fact, my Grandma Gladys's home and stomping grounds. I've known from a very young age that my grandma and I were cut from the same cloth. Perusing over our baby pictures, you might not even tell us apart. I never could have anticipated I would follow in her footsteps in this career pursuit. Grandma Gladys passed away well before I even had nannying on my radar, but callings have a strong undercurrent, shaping our lives even when we don't notice them.

I never intended to be a nanny, but it was in my DNA, part of my legacy passed down through generations. Nannying is in my blood; Nannying is in my history.

Grandma Gladys was the first nanny I ever knew, and there I was, in her home, speaking to a room of professionals in her career. I know she would've been proudly sitting in that front row, in awe of the connections I've made with a community of 16K and counting that I've crafted on Instagram as The Modern Nanny advocating for this profession.

In the end, it wasn't a scam; it was my legacy.

About Sarah Carlisle Stewart

Sarah Carlisle Stewart, known as The Modern Nanny, is a Nanny Culture & Career Coach. After experiencing codependent caregiving that led to burnout and learning boundaries in her nanny career, she created The Modern Nanny in 2020 on the brink of the pandemic, just when the industry would need community most, and has since amassed 16K followers and counting. Passionate about sharing information and fostering connections in a traditionally coworkerless career, she uses humor and commentary to shed light on the unique, and often invisible, shared experiences of domestic workers. Using her background in research prior to her nannying, Sarah developed the Nanny Census Report, surveying nannies every six months on wages and benefits, education and experience, and retention and satisfaction. She has spoken at various webinars for organizations such as the International Nanny Association and the US Nanny Association and events like International Nanny Training Day in Charlotte, North Carolina, and San Diego, CA.

Chapter 6

My Journey to Living the American Dream

By Kim Morgan Smart

My life has been marked by a series of defining challenges, each leaving an indelible imprint on who I am today. I am a woman molded by trials, triumphs, and the unyielding pursuit of a better life for my family.

My story begins on the archipelago island of Saint Vincent and the Grenadines, a beautiful place with a tumultuous history. It is a land of contrasts—lush green landscapes and crystal-clear waters alongside poverty, limited opportunities, and deeply ingrained cultural expectations. My mother was thrust into parenthood at the age of 14. Her strength, determination, and relentless will to provide for me despite her youth inspired me and instilled in me a deep knowing that I was destined for more than the island could provide. A key turning point came after I experienced an attempted assault with my mother by my side. It was then I knew that I could no longer remain in a place that offered little support and few avenues for healing.

In the aftermath of this painful chapter, I made the difficult decision to leave everything I knew behind. I boarded a plane to New York City carrying with me nothing but hope, a desire to escape the suffocating weight of my past, and a dream of building a new life. I was determined to forge my path in a country that promised freedom and opportunity, but I quickly learned that the immigrant experience would come with its own set of hardships.

Immigration and the Early Years—Adapting to a New World

When I arrived in New York City, I was met with an exciting and overwhelming world. The opportunities that had once seemed so distant now felt within reach, but I quickly realized that the road ahead would be fraught with challenges.

As an undocumented immigrant, I was navigating a world that was not designed for people like me. The uncertainty of my legal status hung over every decision, and survival was my immediate priority. My future, and the future of the family I hoped to build, depended on my ability to adapt and find work.

In this new world, I found employment as a nanny. While caring for children came naturally to me, this role was unlike anything I had experienced before. The families I worked for belonged to a class that seemed worlds away from my own struggles. They lived in luxury while I wrestled with the daily realities of financial instability. It was a stark contrast that sometimes felt difficult to reconcile. I was entrusted with their most precious assets—their children—but barely making a livable wage to provide for myself.

Yet, being a nanny became more than just a job; it was an opportunity to engage in a form of cultural exchange that I hadn't anticipated. I brought the values my mother instilled in me—compassion, resilience, and an unwavering commitment to nurture—to every family I worked with. I was able to introduce the children to aspects of my Caribbean upbringing, while, at the same time, being exposed to the cultures, customs, and lifestyles of the families I worked for.

The reality of living in New York City as an undocumented immigrant meant constantly walking a fine line between ambition and survival. With every eviction notice and every bill left unpaid, I was reminded that the opportunities in America came with a steep price. There were many nights when I questioned whether I had made the right decision to leave Saint Vincent, but my determination to succeed outweighed my fears.

Despite the economic hardships, my early years in the U.S. were marked by growth. I found purpose in every family I worked for and every child I nurtured. Through these relationships, I began to see that my role wasn't just about caregiving but about creating bonds, offering guidance, and making a lasting impact on the lives of these children. I also found myself acting as a mentor, sharing the wisdom I had gained from my own life experiences with the parents I worked for.

At the same time, my work allowed me to observe how some families were shaped by their affluence, and I noticed the ways in which parenting expectations were influenced by wealth. This experience reinforced my belief that every child deserves love, guidance, and a stable foundation.

Those early years of immigration were filled with uncertainty, but they also solidified my sense of purpose. I was not just a nanny; I was a woman determined to rise above the limitations that had been placed upon me. The road ahead was long, and the challenges would only increase, but I had already survived so much, and with each day, I was forging a new path for myself and my future family.

Motherhood and Chosen Family

Motherhood has been a dream of mine since I was a little girl; however, I had been told that because of a medical condition, the likelihood of me carrying a child to term was slim. This news was devastating, but in an unexpected turn of events, I became pregnant with my first son, defying the odds that were stacked against me. I was overjoyed by the news but worried about the challenges that lay ahead.

When I immigrated to the U.S., I arrived without any family by my side. It was just me, stepping into a new country, holding onto the hope that I could build a better life. Alone in New York, I had no one to lean on during those critical moments when I needed support the most. Yet, through what I can only describe as divine intervention, the Joslyn family entered my life and became the support system I needed.

I first met them at a volunteer meeting to raise funds for a major political party in Saint Vincent and the Grenadines. Our connection was immediate, grounded in shared values and a deep-seated desire to give back to our homeland. They understood the struggles of immigrant life, and as we worked together to support our community from afar, we developed a bond that would become a lifeline for me.

From the moment I met them, the Joslyns provided the stability and support I had longed for. They became my extended family in every sense of the word, offering guidance, encouragement, and, often, a place to feel the warmth of home.

Their support was unwavering, and they stood by me through countless challenges. With their encouragement, I found the strength to keep moving forward. They celebrated my victories, held me through my

MY JOURNEY TO LIVING THE AMERICAN DREAM

struggles, and reminded me of the resilience that had carried me this far. In them, I found the family I thought I had left behind.

My first pregnancy was anything but smooth. The excitement of becoming a mother was overshadowed by the fear of medical complications. I had been told it could be dangerous, but nothing could have prepared me for what was to come. As I lay in that hospital bed in labor, the excruciating pain was amplified by the sense of impending danger. I thought about my unborn son, and I was determined to stay alive for him. Every ounce of my being focused on survival, on living for the life growing inside me. Thankfully, we both made it through.

The entry into motherhood changed me. It forged a new kind of strength in me that I hadn't known I possessed. I had survived for him and would do everything I could to ensure I provided the life he deserved. Yet, with my precious bundle safely earth-side, I now had to face the challenge of motherhood.

Again, I was blessed with strangers becoming the family I needed. Family N became one of my greatest sources of strength. They were more than just people I worked for; they were my lifeline during one of the most difficult periods of my life. I cared for their three children as a nanny, and they cared for me as a person, not just as the woman they had hired to provide childcare.

But just as I was finding my footing, life threw another curveball my way. I became pregnant with my second son. Instead of joy, I was met with abandonment. My partner, the father of both of my sons, walked out on us. The weight of this abandonment hit me harder than I ever could have imagined. I had thought we were building a life together, but instead, I was left to face the reality of being a single mother of two boys.

The devastation was profound. The emotional toll of being left to fend for myself, with another child on the way, nearly broke me. But once again, Family N became my lifeline. They stood by me when my own partner walked away. They opened their hearts and their home to me, offering a safe space where I could heal and prepare for the arrival of my second son while they were getting ready for the arrival of their own second child. They were there when I didn't have enough for rent, when I didn't know how I would feed my children, and when I questioned how I could raise two boys on my own. They gave me a sense of stability during those fragile months, and their children became like siblings to my own. In their home, I wasn't just the nanny—I was family.

The birth of my second son was another trial, but this time, I was better equipped emotionally. Although I was now a single mother of two, I wasn't alone. Family N continued to support me, and the strength I had gained from surviving the trauma of my first pregnancy carried me through the second. Raising two boys while continuing to care for Family N's children required every ounce of strength I had. Some days felt insurmountable, but the love I had for my sons and the support I received from Family N helped me navigate the storm.

Family N soon welcomed their third child, and together, we continued to thrive as a bonded unit. Looking back, I realize that while I may not have had biological family by my side when I needed them most, I had something just as powerful: a chosen family.

As I navigated the ups and downs of single motherhood, I came to realize that my experience, though challenging, was also a gift. It made me stronger, more determined, and more empathetic. The lessons I learned as a mother and the strength I gained from surviving physical and emotional trials would soon become the foundation of my journey as a business owner.

The Pursuit of Stability

In addition to the many other hardships the pandemic brought, it acted as a magnifying glass, amplifying my financial strains. Yet, amid the chaos and upheaval, my determination to provide a better life for my children crystallized into a fierce pursuit of stability—a pursuit fueled by an unwavering love and a commitment to our future.

I envisioned a life where I could make deliberate choices for myself and my children, allowing me more flexibility and the time to nurture our bond, and I recognized that having control over my schedule would empower me to create the environment I so deeply desired. As I juggled my job and raising my own children, I learned to navigate each day with intention, crafting routines that fostered connection and growth. I rose early each morning, preparing not just meals but also mindsets and setting the tone for the day ahead as I sought to build a foundation for my family.

The experiences I gained working with various families offered invaluable insights into parenting styles, household management, and the myriad ways people navigate the complexities of family life. Each role I took on served as both a lesson and a reflection, pushing me to evaluate my own aspirations for my children and myself. I witnessed different parenting philosophies. Some families emphasized academic excellence, while others celebrated creativity and emotional intelligence. These observations ignited a passionate exploration of the values I wanted to instill in my children. I envisioned raising them with love and creating a legacy they could be proud of.

In our home, I embraced the lessons learned from my various families, combining them with the cultural values and traditions I held dear. Family dinners became sacred moments where we shared food, stories, laughter, and lessons from our days. I made time for open conversations, fostering an environment where my children felt seen and heard, instilling in them a sense of belonging and self-worth.

As I reflected on my journey, it became evident how essential my own transformation was to establishing stability. I had to confront my fears and uncertainties, and as I did, I learned that vulnerability was not a weakness but a step toward growth. Each moment of doubt became a chance to demonstrate to my children that setbacks could be met with determination, allowing them to understand that life's challenges could be overcome through steadfast commitment and creative problem-solving.

Over time, I began cultivating entrepreneurial aspirations to enhance our stability. I recognized the need to build something that could serve as a safety net for our future. I crafted a plan to develop a small business inspired by my experiences: a service that catered to families like those I had worked for, blending elements of nurturing care with cultural experiences. This idea felt like an authentic, natural extension of my journey.

As I navigated the complexities of starting a business, long nights were spent researching, networking, and brainstorming alongside my children. I was determined to involve them in the process, teaching them the importance of hard work, creativity, and the entrepreneurial spirit. Our discussions about dreams and aspirations became family conversations ripe with possibility and excitement.

In every step of this pursuit, I taught them that stability is not merely the absence of struggle but rather the ability to rise, adapt, and grow from challenges. I wanted my children to understand that success is often intertwined with resilience and that each setback can lay the groundwork for something greater.

Rising Through Challenges—Recognition and Achievement

During my journey of motherhood and caregiving, there have been moments that punctuated the narrative and transformed struggles into milestones of recognition and pride. As I diligently honed my skills as a caregiver, pouring my heart into the families I worked with, recognition finally came my way in the form of the International Nanny Association's Nanny of the Year award in 2020.

The nomination itself was incredibly meaningful to me. I was nominated by Sue Downey, Co-Founder of NannyPalooza (a national nanny conference designed by nannies for nannies and nanny-related businesses) and Family D (yet another nanny family that had become like my own). Their son, whom I affectionately call Master Luke, was born on the very day my father passed away—timing I cannot help but see as a gift from above. The nomination for Nanny of the Year and the acknowledgment by the International Nanny Association was a powerful validation of my hard work, passion, and unwavering love for every child who had been entrusted to my care.

Receiving this prestigious award marked a turning point in my professional life—a moment when I felt that my efforts, often hidden in the quiet hours of caring for others, were finally acknowledged. While the world grappled with uncertainty, I found strength and validation in knowing that my commitment to nurturing children had been recognized in such a meaningful way.

This accolade opened doors to high-profile families through Adventure Nannies, a reputed placement agency that matches caregivers with families seeking specialized care. Suddenly, I found myself navigating the expectations of affluent families who held high standards and different perspectives on parenting. With this opportunity came a wave of fresh challenges but also the promise of enriching experiences that would further expand my skills.

Each encounter with these families provided new insights that deepened my commitment to creating a nurturing environment for all children. I learned about diverse parenting philosophies that emphasized emotional intelligence, independence, and self-expression. One family I worked with placed immense value on fostering a love for nature, while another advocated for academic excellence. Each of these experiences expanded my repertoire of caregiving strategies and inspired me to integrate the most effective aspects into my own parenting philosophy.

However, these high-profile families often came with intense expectations and a daunting level of scrutiny. I had to adapt quickly, honing my skills in communication and flexibility. I discovered that being an effective caregiver extended beyond nurturing; it required me to advocate for the children's needs, sometimes in ways that clashed with parental expectations. Navigating these delicate situations tested my resilience but also reinforced my commitment to the children's well-being.

The newfound recognition and opportunities also brought a sense of responsibility. I felt buoyed by the understanding that my journey as a caregiver could inspire others. With each new family, I was determined to embody the values I held dear. As I embraced these roles, I also continued dreaming of a future where I could create my own business that would champion diversity and inclusivity. The lessons learned from high-profile families became valuable tools to leverage to achieve this goal.

Rising through challenges has defined my path toward recognition and achievement. As I reflect on this journey, from the Nanny of the Year Award to the experiences I gained working with high-profile families, I am reminded that every challenge faced and every acknowledgment received is a step toward a legacy of love, resilience, and passion—a path that continues to unfold.

Entrepreneurship—From Nanny to Businesswoman

The seeds of entrepreneurship were planted gradually during my years as a nanny. Working closely with families, I developed a unique understanding of the challenges that new parents face. My role had always extended beyond basic childcare, and as I saw the impact I was making, the idea for *Ambiance Sleep Newborn Care Services* began to take shape in my mind.

The transition from nanny to Newborn Care Specialist (NCS) was natural. With each family I supported, I realized I had a gift: helping parents navigate the early months of parenthood and bond with their newborns. I had witnessed firsthand the transformation that occurred when parents were given the right tools, information, and support, and I knew that I could offer this kind of care to more families if I struck out on my own. With limited resources but an abundance of passion, I took the plunge.

Starting *Ambiance Sleep* was a leap of faith. All I had was my experience, my connections, and a determination fueled by the desire to make life easier for new parents. The families I had worked with over the years became my first advocates. Their recommendations became the foundation of my business. What started as word-of-mouth referrals soon grew into something bigger than I could have ever imagined.

Ambiance Sleep was born with the simple goal of providing high-quality newborn care and parental support. My mission was to bring peace of mind and help parents settle into their roles as caregivers while bonding deeply with their newborns. I didn't just want to give parents advice—I wanted to help them grow into their own confidence and be their partner in this precious time

The early stages of the business were tough. As an immigrant, I was navigating a system that wasn't designed for me. There were legal hurdles, financial obstacles, and the overwhelming task of marketing myself in a highly competitive field. New York City was full of professionals offering various levels of newborn care services, and I had to find a way to stand out.

What set *Ambiance Sleep* apart from other newborn care services wasn't just my technical expertise as an NCS but the deep emotional connection I brought to each family. I had a unique understanding of the struggles that parents faced. I understood the exhaustion that comes with sleepless nights, the fear of doing something wrong, and the pressure to be the 'perfect' parent. My approach was to be an extension of the family, someone they could rely on not just for advice but for empathy, compassion, and understanding.

Soon, I began taking on clients from all walks of life: first-time parents, families with multiples, parents of preemies, and even seasoned parents who just needed an extra hand. My business became a community of support. I built lasting relationships with my clients, and the families I helped didn't just see me as their NCS but as part of their journey. It was through these deep connections that my business continued to thrive.

As my reputation grew, so did the scope of my work. I began offering more than just hands-on care for newborns. I started educating parents on everything from sleep training and feeding schedules to navigating developmental milestones. I ran workshops, offered one-on-one consultations, and expanded my reach to support families nationwide.

Despite the growing success of *Ambiance Sleep*, there were still moments of doubt, but each time I questioned whether I could continue, I thought of the families I had helped and the difference I had made in their lives. That was my motivation.

Looking back, I can see how every challenge prepared me for this journey. My experience as a nanny shaped my understanding of what it takes to provide exceptional care, the financial instability I endured taught me how to be resourceful and resilient, and my role as a mother gave me the empathy and insight that allowed me to connect with families on a personal level.

Today, I am proud of my work and the families I have supported. *Ambiance Sleep* has grown beyond my initial vision, but at its core, it remains rooted in the same values I had when I first started: compassion, trust, and a commitment to helping families thrive during one of the most important times of their lives. Being an entrepreneur, an immigrant, and a single mother shaped me into the person I am today, and I wouldn't trade any of the hardships I've faced for anything.

Finding Balance as a Businesswoman and Single Mother

Balancing motherhood and entrepreneurship was like walking a tightrope. For years, I juggled late nights with newborns and sleep training routines for my clients while also facing the daunting realities of keeping a roof over our heads and food on the table. Yet, no matter how difficult things became, I never allowed my boys to feel the full weight of the financial instability that loomed over us.

At times, the sacrifices seemed too much to bear. I vividly remember trying to decide whether to use my last bit of money to feed my children or pay the rent. No mother should ever have to make that choice, but it was a harsh reality I faced time and time again. It would have been easy to give up, but my boys were my anchor. I couldn't afford to let them see me falter. Their future depended on my ability to rise above the circumstances that threatened to swallow us whole.

While my journey as a business owner was fraught with challenges, nothing compared to the trials of raising two smart black boys in a society that often viewed them through a lens of bias and misunderstanding. I had to be both their shield and their teacher—preparing them for a world that, at times, seemed determined to make their path harder than it needed to be. I taught them how to carry themselves, how to be aware of the prejudices they might face, and how to always remain proud of who they were. My boys are my greatest achievement, and I poured every ounce of my energy into ensuring they received the best education, opportunities, and emotional support.

Despite the chaos, my role as a mother was always my top priority. Every decision I made was driven by the desire to give my sons a life that was stable, filled with opportunity, and free from the struggles I had endured. Their education was of paramount importance, and I remained deeply involved in their schooling, even when the demands of running a business pulled me away from home.

It wasn't until I took Newborn Care Solutions' *Elite to Master's Program* that things started to shift for us. The training I received in this program opened doors I hadn't even known existed. I became equipped with the advanced skills and knowledge needed to provide specialized care at a higher level. The program gave me the confidence to expand *Ambiance Sleep* and connected me with a network that would prove to be life-changing.

One of those opportunities came in the form of a family who, over time, hired me to support two daughters and three grandchildren. What started as just another client relationship turned into a 19-month-long partnership that would transform not only my career but also my life and the lives of my boys. The work was demanding, and while being away from my boys for long stretches of time was one of the hardest sacrifices I have ever had to make, the experience was invaluable.

For the first time, financial stability wasn't merely a concept. I was able to provide for my sons without the constant fear of eviction hanging over us. The opportunity to work with such a high-profile family gave me the financial security I had longed for and allowed me to expand *Ambiance Sleep* in ways I hadn't thought possible.

Yet, the most profound impact was on my boys. The stability that came with this new phase of my career allowed them to focus fully on their education without the shadow of financial worry that had followed us for so long. They saw their mother succeed as a businesswoman who had turned adversity into opportunity. This experience taught them that no matter how hard life may seem, perseverance and hard work can change its trajectory.

Though the road to where we are now was far from easy, every challenge we faced was worth it, and today, my boys and I stand on more solid ground. The uncertainty that once ruled our lives has been replaced with the kind of stability I always dreamed of giving them. The struggles of our past may have been difficult, but they are also the foundation of our strength, and I am eternally grateful for the journey that brought us here.

Resilience, Triumph, and Living the American Dream

Today, I stand as a U.S. citizen, a symbol of perseverance, defying every obstacle that was meant to break me. My life's journey has come full circle, from a young girl growing up on the beautiful but challenging island of Saint Vincent and the Grenadines to a determined woman making a new home in New York City, to an entrepreneur with a thriving business that changes lives.

As I reflect on my journey, I can't help but think of the many families I have supported over the years. My role as a Nanny, and now a Newborn Care Specialist, has been more than my job—it has been my calling. The relationships I have built with clients have brought a deep sense of fulfillment. Each family has been a chapter in my story, and I've had the privilege of walking beside these families as they embark on the most important journey of their lives. Supporting these amazing families has been my joy. Each family I work with reminds me of my own journey and how far I've come.

My boys are the heartbeat of everything I do. As I grew my business and navigated the challenges of entrepreneurship, they stood by me, watching as I fought to create something better for them. Their laughter, their curiosity, and their boundless potential were my motivation. They saw me struggle, but more importantly, they saw me rise. I wanted them to understand that no matter where you come from or what struggles you face, you have the power to shape your own future. Becoming a U.S. citizen solidified that lesson for them—it was proof that despite everything we faced, we could overcome it.

The success of *Ambiance Sleep* isn't measured in wealth or recognition but in the peace I see in the eyes of parents who, after working with me, feel confident and secure in caring for their newborns. It's in the smiles of babies who are nurtured in those critical first months of life and the pride my boys feel knowing that their mother defied every obstacle placed in front of her to create something meaningful and lasting.

Living my passion is about more than the work. I have shown my boys that resilience is not about never falling; it's about always rising, no matter how many times life knocks you down. Today, we are thriving, and I look forward to all that lies ahead, knowing that together, we will continue to rise.

As I move forward, I do so with gratitude for the challenges that shaped me and the opportunities that allowed me to rise. My story is not just one of personal triumph but a testament to the power of resilience, the importance of family—in whatever form they may come—and the belief that with a dream, a little bit of faith, and a whole lot of determination, you can rise above anything.

About Kim Morgan Smart

Kim Morgan Smart is a dual-certified Newborn Care Specialist and Master NCS with over Twenty-Five (25) years of experience in the childcare industry. As a seasoned expert in infant care and sleep coaching, Kim has become a trusted guide for new and expecting parents nationwide. Through her personalized and compassionate approach, she empowers families to embrace the newborn phase with confidence, ensuring their infants are well-supported and thriving.

As the founder of Ambiance Sleep Newborn Care Services, an in-home business based in New York serving clients nationwide, Kim is dedicated to providing evidence-based guidance and customized care that aligns with each family's unique needs. Inspired by her own journey as a devoted mother to two black boys, a caregiver, and an educator, she developed a three-step approach to establish healthy sleep patterns and ease the transition into parenthood. Drawing on her extensive training and expertise, Kim combines cutting-edge research with practical strategies, helping parents create a nurturing environment for both their babies and themselves.

Chapter 7

More Than "Just a Nanny"

By Emma Hughes

"Hi, I'm Emma. I'm a nanny."

Have *you,* a single and eligible and childless young woman in her prime, ever rolled up to a first date with car seats in the back, a portable potty in the trunk, and snot on your pants? No? Well, me neither, because that would mean I'd actually gone on a date in the past five years. Alas, I have gone on *zero* dates and have had very little of anything resembling a life outside of work up until very recently, but you get my point. Don't worry, I still have time before my self-imposed 27-year deadline inspired by Pride and Prejudice (the 2004 Keira Knightley version, obviously).

Here's another Jane Austen-ism for you: It is a universally acknowledged truth that if your job has an "appreciation day," you're probably not getting paid enough. Every September, nannies get a *whole week*. National Nanny Recognition Week runs from the 22nd to the 28th and involves gift cards, giveaways, and tokens of appreciation from agency owners and employers alike. It's a time of tagging your nanny friends in every single social media giveaway and crossing your fingers that you'll receive swag bags galore. It's also a time of dropping hints to clueless employers (AKA busy parents) like, "Oh, my weekend plans? Going out to lunch with some other nannies in honor of NNRW." Wink wink, nod nod, please give me a gift card or book me a massage (or at the very least, write a Thank-You note).

For over five years, I lived and breathed nannying. When introducing myself, I'd say, "Hi, I'm Emma. I'm a nanny." I worked full-time, clocking 40 to 50+ hours a week, not just caring for children but also tackling the mountains of invisible labor that come with keeping a household running smoothly. I coordinated calendars, researched swim programs and hockey lessons, and kept the fridge filled and the pantry stocked. I witnessed first steps (if you're a parent reading this, actually, no, I never saw any firsts *ever*), learned to make an out-of-this-world strawberry galette, polished a repertoire of lullabies, and became a boo-boo kisser extraordinaire. I made sure we never ran out of diapers or wipes, planned nutritious meals, led the charge on starting solids and potty training, kept track of milestones, navigated behavioral challenges, and made sure the kids spent as much time outside (and as little time on screens) as possible. I've spent hours creating Christmas gift wish lists, stitched ripped stuffies back together, inventoried freezers of breast milk, cleaned up countless potty accidents, and once, I even had to climb through a family's guest bedroom window when I accidentally locked myself out (with their 10-month-old daughter inside) after taking their dog out to pee.

I spent years in the thick of early childhood, starting my first position with a three-month-old and a three-year-old in 2019. I stayed with them for two and a half years, even going so far as to temporarily move halfway across the country to help them settle into their new home in Wisconsin in the spring of 2021. By the time I left, that three-month-old was a

MORE THAN "JUST A NANNY"

running, talking, and usually singing toddler, aged two and three-quarters (and if you asked her, the "three-quarters" was *not* to be left out). The boy who was once just a wee three-year-old? He started Kindergarten that fall.

After two months of getting the children settled, the household set up, and 95% of the boxes unpacked, I left my short stint in the Midwest with absolutely no love lost for the region. Now, before any midwesterners yell at me (just kidding, you would never yell; you're too midwestern nice for such shenanigans), I am a born and bred Mainer who has never lived more than an hour from the ocean. I'm sure *some people* can stand to be landlocked, but one of the big things I learned in this formative adventure was that *I* am not one of them. Dear Wisconsin, you do love your cheese, and for *that,* you have my utmost respect. But you are hot and swampy in the summer and a freezing tundra in the winter, and filled with more cows than people all year long, and I was absolutely not sad to see myself out.

Upon my prodigal daughter's return to the great state of Maine, I jumped right into my next assignment. Wash, rinse, repeat. My position began with an 18-month-old and a six-months-pregnant Mom Boss. They were leaving the gender a surprise, and I was beside myself with excitement. Just over three months later, after being on baby-watch for weeks (at first, we thought the baby would come early, but the due date came and went and went some more and we were all getting just a wee bit impatient), I was awoken one night at three AM and told by a very calm and pleasant Mom that, "My water just broke, but take your time getting here. No rush!" 45 minutes later I got another call as I was pulling off the highway, this time it was Dad and he was, well, slightly less calm. "How far away are you?" he wanted to know, and "We're going to get in the car and pull out as you pull in." In the background I could hear Mom's low groans, less than two hours into active labor after weeks of waiting. I knew, then and there, that this child was going to be a fun one (and oh boy, was I right). I had barely gotten settled into the guest room, not even twenty minutes into Sleepless in Seattle, when my phone dinged with a text. Baby girl had been born not even five minutes after getting to the hospital, the midwife wasn't even in the room. In fact, she'd very nearly been born in the car. But she was here! And she was a girl! I had Meg Ryan and Tom Hanks on my laptop, a baby monitor showing the sleeping 21-month-old upstairs, their dog curled at my feet, a new child I'd get to care for and a new day dawning. Life was good.

I loved being a full-time nanny. I'd hear friends bemoan their days full of Zoom calls and emails and "Let's circle back!" and feel endlessly smug that *I* was getting paid to read Frog & Toad and spend hours hunting for seashells at the beach. Sure, my day also included getting accidentally peed on and carrying a melting-down toddler, literally kicking and screaming, from the playground to the car. But those things didn't phase me, and they couldn't come close to the house of horrors that is the corporate world. My friends can keep their spreadsheets and powerpoints and slack threads. I'll be over here going for hikes and having tea parties and not sharing a breakroom microwave with someone who thinks it's okay to reheat fish.

Unfortunately, people love to diminish nannying. How hard can your job be? You "just play with kids all day." *Insert buzzer noise here.* No. Incorrect. False.

Whenever you talk to teachers or nannies or really anyone in the early childhood space, they'll always tell you the same thing. The kids are rarely, *if ever,* the problem; the parents are. Now, I've been fortunate to work for some amazing parents, and this is absolutely not a dig on any of them, but the point remains. Kids, I can handle. Kids are predictably unpredictable. I expect a two year old to have a meltdown. I expect a baby to cry. Adults, on the other hand? A bit more complicated. Tensions can rise when your professional insight clashes with parental preference. It's not your average 9 to 5 where you can just walk out the door at the end of your assigned shift; you're at the mercy of busy parents and the whims of traffic patterns. You can't leave until you're relieved, and it stinks. Lines get blurred; it can be hard to balance being personable, retaining your own life, and toeing the line of professionalism while being so intimately acquainted with the inner workings of a family and home. Nannies see and hear a lot. We know when Mom and Dad are fighting, when Grandma has outstayed her welcome, when they're trying for another baby. If they're successful, if they're not. We file away idiosyncrasies and pet peeves, preferences and anxieties. We do our best to navigate it all with professionalism and grace, but goodness gracious, people are just plain hard to deal with sometimes.

You see, the kids are the easy part. "You just play with kids?" Well, yes, I do. It's a really cool part of the job. But it's *part* of the job. A very small part, actually. Remember the laundry list of responsibilities I detailed earlier? While only some of them were written in my contracts, I ended up doing all of them at one point or another. It's the hazard of the job when the job is caring for someone's child and, by extension, being the backbone of an entire household.

When written down in black and white, a nanny's job duties can seem fairly straightforward. Contracts often include something along the lines of: "Care of the children, including but not limited to: preparing nutritious meals, diapering/toileting, maintaining basic hygiene, ensuring development through outings and activities, etc." But with each of those black and white tasks, there is an endless sea of gray. It's hard to put into words the weight of it all. *Will last year's snowsuit fit, or will we need to order another? Did I get the stain out of that shirt? Did their Mom schedule their annual exam, or was I supposed to? Have we restocked on diapers lately? I wonder if we need to get the next size up. They'll only eat off the blue plate, not the orange one. Should we plan a playdate with that girl down the street? I wonder if I should ask about getting him assessed by a speech therapist, but I don't want to stress the parents out. Dad has court this week; did anyone remember to grab his suits from the cleaners? Trash day is Thursday, so I need to empty the diaper pail.* And so it goes, on and on and on and on. Domestic labor is systemically undervalued, *invisible* and *mental* labor especially so.

Nannying is one of the most unique industries, with unfathomable disparity between the haves and the have-nots. It's entirely unregulated. There are some baseline qualifications, like CPR and First Aid training and ideally prior childcare experience. There are some families who view the work as "glorified babysitting" and seek to lowball pay accordingly, while others are willing to pay a premium for quality care. Those with means will often have a roster full of nannies and childcare industry specialists; from Newborn Care Specialists to travel nannies to home educators and beyond, spending hundreds of thousands of dollars a year on private childcare alone. And while I do know many nannies earning six-figure salaries, they are unfortunately the exception, not the rule. For most nannies, there's an ongoing battle for fair and legal pay, and the standardization of benefits such as health care stipends and paid time off. Most industries have the luxury of an HR department, while most nannies have to do everything themselves. Not to mention that your workplace? It's someone's *home*. Your job duties? Just about as nuanced as it can get.

The price of private, in-home childcare "skyrocketed" during the pandemic. Some families seeking to limit exposure were concerned about sending their kids to daycares and schools, while others simply couldn't cope with the unreliability due to constant closures. It seemed like every family was seeking a nanny, and there simply weren't enough nannies to go around. For the first time, possibly ever, nannies were realizing that they held the power. Don't want to put me on payroll? That's okay. I can find a family that will. Offering $20/hr for three kids? Another family is offering $30/hr for one.

Now, to be fair to families, it is *rough* to be a parent in the land of the free. We need childcare reform of the highest level, and we needed it like 20 years ago. When compared to countries like France and their top-notch specially staffed Creches or Denmark and their guaranteed placement of children 0-6 within their public childcare system, America is living in the dark ages. Not to mention the utter and complete lack of proper maternity and paternity leave. Parents today face countless challenges, and the cost of living just keeps climbing. Many parents were left with sticker shock when confronted with the comprehensive costs of becoming household employers, "Nannies make *how much*?!" Parents everywhere were realizing what we've been trying to say all along: childcare is *work*. It's hard work, and those providing it should be compensated accordingly. But here's the thing: the pandemic didn't singlehandedly create a childcare crisis; it just brought to light a system that was broken to begin with. Every family and child is entitled to quality care, but not every family can afford (or should employ) a nanny. I digress. Soapbox sermon over.

In the fall of 2024, I resigned from the full-time position I'd held for over two years because of something that runs rampant in our industry: caregiver burnout. The byproduct of an unregulated and undervalued industry, caregiver burnout is the reason many nannies leave the field entirely. This is often a highly emotional decision, as most nannies do what they do *because* they love it. There's a certain element of "calling" to this career, and you don't last long without it. A good nanny is a wearer of many hats and often has many "unrelated" passions and interests outside of work (we are, after all, actual people at the end of the day). But the common denominator is usually this: a genuine love for children and childhood, a passion for their growth and development and the role we can play within that. To put it simply, a good nanny is a good childcare provider because they *care*.

It's hard work to care so much. It's exhausting to carry the weight of an entire household on your shoulders. It's stressful to know that *you* are the piece of the puzzle that allows your employers to do *their* jobs. How can you call out sick when your boss has a day full of surgeries booked? How can you take time off when they can't find anyone to cover you? When there's no grandparent waiting in the wings, ready and willing to be called in? It's easy to allow your job to become your identity. Many great nannies are natural-born givers; it's often how we find ourselves in this industry to begin with. But if we're not careful with all that giving, eventually, we'll realize that we've simply got nothing left.

What do you do when the crushing weight of your own love and compassion and dedication to doing your job well comes crashing down on you? What do you do when you realize you're tired and depressed and no amount of appreciation weeks or social media giveaways or massages will fix it?

Well, if you're me, you burn it all down. No, really. You let one final straw break the camel's back, you admit that you're not doing well, and you recognize that the definition of insanity is doing the same thing over and over and expecting a different result. You submit your resignation (reminder: there is no HR department, so "submitting your resignation" is really just you and your Mom Boss crying in the living room while the children you've revolved your life around for two years play, loud and oblivious, in the other room). You light everything you thought you knew about yourself, your job, and your identity on fire.

You spend a year having a properly spectacular quarter-life crisis. You go on an "Eat Pray Love" three-week solo adventure through Europe. You say, "If not now, when?" After having almost no life outside of work for four years, you make up for lost time. You rack up airline miles and somehow find yourself on 18 planes in the span of 10 months. You realize you didn't actually hate nannying (a relief), you just needed a change of pace. Travel nannying, temp nannying, newborn care, postpartum support; you do it all. You spend a month in South Carolina for work and form a respectfully terrified relationship with the neighborhood alligator. You visit friends, near and far. You eat s'mores on a couch in the woods of North Carolina with a friend who was a stranger not even one year prior. You realize all of your best friendships have been born out of this industry, the one that so often feels like the Wild West. You realize there's something exceedingly beautiful about the fact that this thing that has taken and taken from you has also given in equal measure.

You realize that you've spent the past five years introducing yourself as "Hi, I'm Emma. I'm a nanny." You wonder what you are if *not* that. What parts and pieces of you are in there, waiting, worth bearing the weight of your identity. What might be worth moving up in the priority list? You spend a beautifully, painfully messy year being alive. There are a lot of high highs and a lot of low lows. You ask lots of questions, go on adventures, and do lots of soul-searching. You have identity crisis after identity crisis. You send many late-night texts to friends saying, "I don't know what to do! I don't know what I want to be when I grow up!" You sit on your couch one afternoon writing this story, and you realize you don't have an ending. After all, how could you? The story is still being written. It's popular belief that all stories have to have endings, but if you'll allow it, I'd like to "end" mine with an introduction instead:

EMMA HUGHES

"Hi, I'm Emma! I love Jesus and being by the ocean and cooking and chocolate croissants. I read a lot. No really, like *a lot!* (87 books so far this year, as a matter of fact!) If you ever need a romance or fantasy recommendation, I'm your girl. I love a love story, and I'm faithfully (and not at all anxiously) waiting for the day when I get to have one of my own. I love to travel, and I'm not afraid to go alone. I actually *love* traveling alone; I love *being* alone. I'm just not quite as fond of being lonely. I'm a collector of knowledge and a lover of history, and I've never met a museum audio tour I didn't love. I'm from Maine, and I really love it here. I love watching the wildflowers bloom in the spring, going for swims in the cold Atlantic on a hot summer's day, and going for hikes to admire the changing leaves in the fall. You'll notice I've omitted winter because, frankly, the older I get, the more it sucks.

I have four cats, and I know I shouldn't have a favorite, but I do, and his name is Simon. Some may say I have too many houseplants, but I think those people are wrong. I love going for walks in the woods, watching sunsets, and the feel of grass under bare feet. I saw the northern lights three times this year and cried like a baby every time. I've been getting braver recently about trying new foods. For example, I learned that the hype was real; kale is actually really good!

All my friends are coupled or married, and I dream of the day when I have a husband and a home filled with my own children running underfoot. Some days, it feels like I have so much love inside of me, just waiting to be poured out, and I don't know how to cope with the pressure of it all. Until my motherhood chapter begins, I plan to keep spreading that love out on other people's families. I wear a lot of jumpsuits, I love a twirly dress, and these days my favorite color is pink. I love daisies and lupines, and I think I want to grow a flower garden next year! Simon and Garfunkel are probably my favorite artists of all time, but I love Taylor

Swift too. I'm always down to go thrifting, and I know the best spot in town for tacos.

Oh, what do I do for work, you ask? I hold little hands and even littler hearts. I help households run smoothly and create margin for busy families. I'm a singer, a dancer, and an animated story reader. I'm a baby whisperer and a toddler wrangler. I'm an amateur chef and a five-star chauffeur and I have unbelievably extensive knowledge of cars and trucks and things that go. I can distinguish a backhoe from an excavator in three seconds flat. I have a favorite dinosaur (Dreadnoughtus; what an epic name). I can recite "Giraffes Can't Dance" from memory, and I have a tattoo of Frog and Toad. I'm Emma. I'm a wearer of many hats, a woman of many talents, a container of multitudes, and I'm a nanny.

About Emma Hughes

While her "Eat, Pray, Love" AKA "catch flights, not feelings" year is winding down, Emma would like to remind you that you don't have to wait until middle age to have a crisis. Quarter-life will do just fine. Emma currently works part-time as a nanny, part-time as a postpartum doula, and full-time as a human being. She lives in her beloved home state of Maine and has found that one of the secrets to life is always having a trip planned. She can be found on Instagram @themainenanny and is highly considering offering cash incentives to anyone who can successfully set her up with her future husband.

Chapter 8

Adventure is a Mindset

By James Austin V

The five-year-old asks me, "Is this a two-adventure day or a three-adventure day?"

What do you want it to be?

"A three-adventure day!"

Let's go!

At the time, we were on an island in the South Pacific, but the kids I worked with learned this question in their own backyards. They also learned that "adventure" is a mindset rather than an event or far-away location. Adventure doesn't mean you did the hardest thing you've ever done, tried a food you've never heard of, or suffered and triumphed. Adventure is a lens to turn the everyday into the exceptional, to keep the fountain of curiosity flowing, to teach self-reliance and interconnectedness, and to choose fun and kindness over grumpiness. One of the other kids I worked with once asked, "James, what do you hate more than anything? Besides bad attitudes."

I'm the daughter of a librarian and a blacksmith, so I grew up immersed in stories and ready to build and fix. I carried those stories and ethos with me to the stream on my small Mid-Atlantic sheep farm and built imaginary worlds with my friends and neighbors. What we saw on the few VHS movies we owned took flight in our woods and fields. That imagination carried me to independently study abroad in Spain at 15 years old and on to Dartmouth College, Ski Patrol, firefighting, leading trips for high schoolers in Costa Rica, Chile, Ecuador, Australia, France, and Italy, classroom teaching in Maine and Colorado, managing projects for an engineering company in Seattle, and running a summer camp in Shanghai. None of that varied resume would have been possible without my foundation between the pages of so many beloved books and a belief that with a spoonful of sugar, anything is possible. Now, imagine picking all your favorite magical items from the pages of your most beloved books and using them to add a little sparkle and a few lessons to the lives of children. That's how I felt as an Adventure Nanny.

Mary Poppins' carpet bag? I had it—though perhaps not quite so bottomless…and not as floral. My bag was always full of surprises to pass the time, spark creativity, and inspire kindness. I always had gems for a treasure hunt, pens and paper for thank-you notes and drawing games, a digital recorder for capturing stories, something that glowed in the dark, and lots and lots of snacks. At my seaside interview with one family, the little boy wasn't too sure about meeting a new nanny. I pulled a pencil and paper out, and he got curious, and once he was looking over my shoulder I said, "Guess what animal I'm drawing." A half-giraffe, a third-of-a-fox, and a few octopus tentacles later, we were fast friends. We kept playing that game all across the world for the next two years. In England, New Zealand, Hong Kong, Switzerland, Thailand, and more, we always knew how to make fun. Why did I pack an audio recorder when any smartphone has a recorder app? As a nanny, I had the luxury to never depend on phones as a form of entertainment and engagement. As any adult knows, if you pick up your phone to do one specific thing, it isn't too long before you're 30 minutes into something else, or several something elses. I could go backward in time with less technology and more imagination.

Aladdin's lamp? I had that, too, but not in the way you might think. As a nanny, I had access to all the supplies I needed to support an active learning environment. The children's wishes weren't so readily answered. One misconception about the children I worked with is that they must have all been spoiled brats. Despite their material wealth, not one was spoiled in behavior, but their "normal" was a far cry from almost every child in the world. The kids would beg to fly commercial instead of on their family's private planes because they had heard on commercial planes everyone gets their own TV screen, and that's what they wanted. It sounded much better to them than having to negotiate with siblings and cousins about what to watch on the big screen in the plane's living room. With another family, I cared for a child with a chronic illness who was constantly tasked with educating his peers and adults about his needs. I would have taken one of those Genie wishes to give him a life free of disease, but no cure exists (yet). While I couldn't grant the wish to banish illness, or for us all to fly Southwest to get our own TVs, I had more than three wishes to get what the kids needed to learn about their interests. For a kid who loved the sea, we would be in aquariums and museums, surfing and snorkeling, and reading bedtime stories about the ocean. I wish every child could have that gift—the resources to follow their passions.

Hermione's time turner? As a nanny, I didn't need one—I already had the gift of time. Time to anticipate and plan. In 2024, a viral post warned that hurrying children leads to long-term anxiety. Though the post was a slight misinterpretation of a study done in the 1980s, the ethos sent me straight back to my nannying days and the sense of gratitude I felt for having plenty of time to help kids build independence. I wasn't there to do it for them; I was there to provide the tools and systems to build critical thinking and planning skills. We didn't have to rush. For a season, I helped care for an infant, and in doing so, I got to spend time with the grandparents. I would strap on the baby carrier and go with Grandpa on daily walks through the redwoods. This time spanning generations was priceless. I loved the shade of the giant trees, the soft ground, the warmth of the baby on my chest, and Grandpa's stories from a time long, long ago. Our walks were a living fairy tale, and they slowed time down in a way that is rare to access in our modern day. I still quote Grandpa when I start something long or difficult, "Small steps, long way." This wealth of time was a far cry from my time as a classroom teacher, a setting in which there is never enough time to give each young person the dedicated attention they all deserve. Imagine you had all the time you wish you did to spend with your kids and let your creativity run wild. That was the time I had.

C.S. Lewis' magic wardrobe? We could go through those doors any time into a world of imagination and creation. Having the time to follow the imagination of a child is an opportunity to travel to other worlds. The famous 1968 Land and Jarman study, which asked children and adults to come up with different uses for paperclips, showed that our thinking often narrows as we age. Understanding the power of imagination is one of my foundational values as a caregiver. Once, a family decided not to take me on a vacation halfway around the world. The private island they were visiting promised childcare, and it would give me a couple weeks off. A few days into the trip, I got the call: "Can you get on a plane and meet us as soon as possible?" "Of course." The island's caregivers were passive, not engaging the kids, and spending time on their phones. The call was unexpected but gratifying. It gave me a sense of recognition that there is value to the time I put in to inspire imagination and curiosity. Once I got there, we built extravagant sandcastles, played "soccer" with some extra made-up rules, picked up and admired every shell on the beach, and tried every fruit we'd never seen before. I also got lost on a long trail run and was out for 16 miles rather than 6 (how big can this island be??), but I was back in time for dinner with no one the wiser except my aching legs.

Neverland? Well, we did fly quite a bit, though we used planes and helicopters rather than pixie dust. I leaped at the chance to take off in the cockpit of a 767 and slept in a queen bed in the sky on the way back from the South Pacific. Once, after a spur-of-the-moment short helicopter flight, we ended up at a gathering where, during the round of introductions, Ira Glass said, "I've danced with Yoko Ono, and this is the weirdest event I've ever been to." The six-year-old then stood on his chair and introduced himself to a room filled with adults with a calm beyond his years. "Never grow up" is the creed of Peter Pan, but as a nanny, my cause was to support growth and to care for the children, keeping in mind who they would grow to be someday.

Which brings me to the cloak of invisibility. The puzzle is how to honor creating ease in the family's life without taking away the important work of being a child. Doing everything for a child just to keep yourself busy and feeling "useful" will create a dependent, spoiled kiddo who expects to be waited on indefinitely. My favorite magic to make was the kind I didn't get credit for, being able to anticipate what was needed to make family time without me frictionless. Doing the behind the scenes work that pushed the kids to shine on the stage of their own lives. I love getting updates from my former charges—some are in college now, and all are thriving. They care about others, about making the world a better place. I send them pictures from when they were tiny and tell them how proud I hope they are of themselves and how excited I am to see them accomplish even more, with big hearts and thinking brains and a well of generosity and optimism.

Were there James Bond movie moments? Absolutely! Eating fresh calamari in Porto Fino and swimming back to the boat. Always driving straight onto the tarmac to board the plane. An unlimited cheese budget in Paris. A private tour of the War Rooms in London. Scuba diving with former Navy Seals to recover a lost item from a yacht. Night markets in Bangkok. An evasive driving course with the security team. Helicopter rides to one picnic lunch on a pink sand beach and another in hanging glacial lakes in New Zealand…okay, any time there was a helicopter involved. And yet, these moments were few and far between and paled in comparison to the adventure of daily life. The laughter on the way to school drop off, cheering at sports games, seeing a child stand up on a surfboard for the first time, helping them learn to spell their own name, making handmade valentines, cooking meals together, helping plan a surprise for mom or dad. Or hearing a child say, "You're not my best friend anymore. You're family." No James Bond moment is better than being a safe place for a child.

I always want a three-adventure day (or a five-adventure day…), so what's the best? A helicopter picnic, exploring glow worm caves, and a horseback ride on the beach? British cream tea, a castle tour, Stonehenge? First tram at Jackson Hole, ice skating, star-gazing? Or is it a homemade breakfast, a note in the lunchbox, and a walk in the neighborhood? Surfing, sand castles, and bedtime stories? The seemingly extraordinary can be an awful day in poor company, and the mundane can be legendary alongside people you enjoy. At the end of the day, it wasn't about the carpet bag, the time-turner, the wardrobe, the pixie dust, or the cloak so much as it was about being together.

I learned just as much from the children I cared for as I was able to teach them. As Carl and Russell remind us in the movie Up: "Adventure is out there!" And adventure is also in all of us, if we know how to open our senses and our hearts to live kindly and boldly.

About James Austin V

James Austin V was raised on a sheep farm in Maryland. She graduated Dartmouth College with her BA in Spanish and Education in 2007. She worked as a classroom teacher, firefighter, ski patroller, summer camp director, adventure nanny, and nurse before finding her way to midwifery. In 2021 she graduated Seattle University with her Doctor of Nursing Practice as a Certified Nurse Midwife. She is also an International Board Certified Lactation Consultant. She currently works in a hospital-based group midwifery practice in Tucson, AZ. James has farm-raised work ethic, big city savvy, world-wide experience and never-ending curiosity and believes in the wonder and importance of childhood from the backyard to the far corners of the planet.

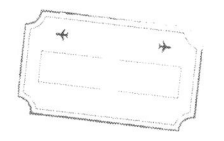

Chapter 9

Mom Boss Magic

By Reagan Fulton

They say it takes a village to raise a child. But what about raising a dream? It turns out that takes a village, too. And mine? Well, it was overflowing with badass women who showed me that motherhood wasn't a detour on the road to ambition but a freaking fast track.

But before we get to all that "mom boss" magic, let's rewind to the beginning, shall we? Picture this: a little Reagan, seven years old, twirling around in her backyard with dandelion crowns and grass-stained knees, already dreaming of motherhood. It was the only answer I ever gave when grown-ups asked that age-old question, "What do you want to be when you grow up?" A mommy. Simple, pure, unwavering.

Growing up in the Midwest, in a conservative homeschool community, my vision of motherhood was straight out of a Little House on the Prairie book, with a dash of Veggie Tales thrown in for good measure. Think homemade bread, gingham dresses, and maybe a "Silly Song" or two while scrubbing the floors. Okay, maybe not *exactly* like that, but you get the idea. I was surrounded by loving, dedicated moms who poured their hearts into creating magical childhoods for their kids. And I'm eternally grateful for the joyful, playful foundation they helped build for me.

Almost all the moms I knew were stay-at-home-homeschooling moms, their worlds a whirlwind of unit studies, piano lessons with siblings, and bandaging scraped knees after epic games of "Capture the Flag" at the park with the local co-op. It was a beautiful way to grow up, surrounded by family and a strong sense of community. But the idea of a working mom? Balancing a career with the demands of raising kids? It was an exception rather than a rule for most of the families I encountered growing up.

The first time I remember consciously thinking about what motherhood looked like beyond this traditional framework came courtesy of my incredible aunt. A teacher, writer, and journalist, she effortlessly shattered the mold. She returned to the classroom full-time after having her two boys, proving that motherhood and a fulfilling career weren't mutually exclusive. When I was twelve years old, she invited me down to New Orleans to join her at the first of two t(w)een travel writing workshops that she was organizing with a colleague through the prestigious private school she taught at in the heart of New Orleans' Garden District. I spent the week getting to explore The Big Easy, falling in love with it effortlessly as I walked the worn and weathered streets of Jackson Square, met French Quarter residents, and learned from incredible writers and artists about to tell their stories well and truthfully. I also got to see a new perspective on motherhood.

You see, to execute this incredible experience—bringing together 12 young women from across the country for a week of learning, travel, and creativity—she had to step away from her typical "motherhood" role. Or at least, that's how I saw it at the time. We were immersed in the vibrant energy of the French Quarter, staying in a hotel, and the boys came down once or twice for quick visits to get in some mom and cousin face time with them while I was in town.

But even with the shift in focus, she remained present, engaged, and wholeheartedly dedicated to those young aspiring writers. Years later, I realized that this wasn't abandoning motherhood at all. It was an act of courage, a testament to her ability to nurture and inspire beyond the boundaries of her own family. It was a powerful demonstration of the multifaceted nature of motherhood, a truth that resonated deep within me.

Watching her navigate both roles with grace and determination planted a seed in my young mind, a seed that would take years to fully blossom. It would require the nurturing and support of other incredible women, including my own mother, who bravely stepped out of "full-time homeschooling mom" mode and returned to nursing school while raising four teenagers. Their examples and their unwavering belief in themselves and their dreams helped shape my understanding of what motherhood truly means.

Years later, there I was, a full-fledged nanny, knee-deep in diapers and snack time negotiations. I loved being part of other families' lives, helping those amazing mamas chase their dreams. But somewhere between the bedtime stories and the playground adventures, I'd swallowed this sneaky little lie: that pursuing my own ambitions meant I couldn't be a "good" mom. Like *somehow* those two things were mutually exclusive, like oil and water or glitter and black leggings.

It wasn't just a fleeting thought, either. This belief was so ingrained that it even influenced my college trajectory. You see, I had started out as a Computer Engineering major, all bright-eyed and blonde-haired, full of ambition, ready to take on the tech world—I loved being one of the only girls in my class, ready to take on the boys. But then, the reality of a demanding research career hit me (no doubt helped by the external messaging I was receiving around me).

How could I possibly balance the demands of a career in tech research with my dreams of motherhood?

So, I did what any self-sabotaging college student would do: I switched my major to early childhood education, convincing myself it was a more "mom-friendly" path.

I now recognize how my fear of not being a good mom once held me back from chasing my dreams. But the thing about dreams is they don't die; sometimes, they just evolve. And sometimes, that evolution involves crossing paths with people who will completely redefine what you thought was possible.

That's exactly what happened when I landed this nanny gig with a mom boss who would totally rock my world (for those who *aren't* chronically online nannies, mom boss, or "MB," stands for a mom who is also your nanny employer). This wasn't your average mom. She was an executive project manager working in construction. Not only would she head out to the office looking ready to tackle a boardroom (with a hard hat in tow), but she was also negotiating million-dollar deals one minute and wiping sticky hands the next. She was a total badass, and I was instantly in awe.

This woman was different from any "working mom" I'd ever encountered. Fiercely ambitious and driven to succeed in her career, yes, but also deeply devoted to her children—gentle, silly, present, fun, and kind. She'd actually moved her family from Austin, Texas, back to her hometown of Cincinnati to build that village that she knew was essential for thriving as both a mother and an ambitious career woman. It takes a village, after all, to raise a child, to raise a mother, to raise a dream. And she was consciously creating hers.

That's where I came in. She hired me because she wanted her kids to experience those early years together, exploring the city and creating memories instead of being separated in different daycare classes.

From the very first interview, I knew this was something special. She was intentional about building a life that allowed her to be fully present with her kids while also kicking ass in the boardroom *and* on the construction site. It was inspiring to witness, and it definitely planted a seed in my mind that maybe, just maybe, I could have both, too.

It wasn't long after I started with this family that I found out I was pregnant with my own son, starting the real journey of discovering what motherhood truly meant to me—not just what I thought it would look like. As I navigated those early days of motherhood, my amazing boss became more than just an employer; she became a mentor, a friend, a fellow traveler on this crazy journey, and someone who understood the delicate dance of raising both babies and dreams.

Her example, her friendship… it wasn't long before those subtle hints turned into not-so-subtle nudges. She saw me drowning in the depths of postpartum depression and anxiety, losing myself in the all-consuming role of "mom." And bless her soul; she wasn't about to let me disappear.

She saw me as more than just a mom, though I was rocking that gig, let me tell you. But she also saw the dreams simmering beneath the surface, the passions waiting to be reignited. And with a gentle but firm hand, she pushed me to rediscover who I was outside of motherhood, to chase those dreams with the same fierceness I brought to diaper changes and bedtime battles. She was showing me, through her words and actions, what it means to raise a mother.

And let me tell you, that nudge? That was a life-changer. I'll forever be grateful for her unwavering belief in me and her ability to see through the facade I put on of being the ultimate supermom, even when I couldn't see through it myself.

I slowly began the process of finding myself again. I rediscovered my passion for photography, that old flame, finding joy in capturing those genuine moments of human connection. I went back to painting and drawing, my hands remembering the rhythm of creating. I dove headfirst into books, eager to soak up new ideas and perspectives. And I reconnected with nature, finding peace in the quiet strength of those towering trees and the untamed beauty of the wilderness. Piece by piece, I was coming back to myself, feeling more vibrant and alive with each step.

Then, bam! Covid hit. In spring 2020, the world turned upside down. By this time, I had found myself working for another incredible woman who was a financial executive at a Fortune 500 company. We're talking commanding boardrooms, charming investors, and even ringing the New York Stock Exchange bell—the whole shebang.

We were the perfect yin and yang when it came to raising our boys. With schools closed and the world in lockdown, our day became filled with more than just permission slips, homework, and schedules. It was full-on virtual schooling, crafting epic lesson plans that would make Pinterest explode, documenting every adorable (and not-so-adorable) moment for posterity—you know, so people would know what we did during "the dark days" of the Covid-19 pandemic.

She was amazing, totally killing it in the boardroom, shattering glass ceilings, and inspiring women everywhere. But with all that on her plate, she needed support on the home front. That's where I came in. I became the backbone of the household, the one who ensured everything ran smoothly while she focused on conquering the corporate world. I organized the chaos, tackled the never ending task of decluttering toys, and kept those little humans happy and engaged.

Which, let's be honest, sometimes meant embracing the chaos. Muddy puddles? Bring 'em on. Tree climbing adventures? Yes, please! Those boys were wild and free, and I loved every minute of it. Of course, she had her limits. Baby wipes for those muddy feet were non-negotiable. (Hey, a mom's gotta have her standards, right?) But she loved that her boys were getting that outdoor, messy play they needed, even if she didn't have to witness it firsthand.

We were a team, a village, each bringing our unique strengths to the parenting table. It was a powerful reminder that kids benefit from having different types of adults in their lives. And it showed me just how much I was capable of. Here I was, this nanny/household manager, brainstorming business ideas with a Fortune 500 executive, offering parenting advice, and feeling like I was actually making a difference. Who knew?

And conquer she did! While I was busy navigating the chaos of virtual learning and keeping those little humans alive, she was busy girl-bossing her way to a massive promotion. We're talking shattering glass ceilings, taking names, and ultimately, relocating the whole family overseas. (Talk about a plot twist!) But hey, that's what happens when you're a total rockstar at your job, right? And I was happy to be a part of her success, even if it meant saying goodbye and sending them off on their next adventure.

When she told me about their move, we cried together for a long time. Not only had our boys become best friends who spent all day, every day together, but we had become friends as well. Sure, I was thrilled for her, but there was also this undeniable sadness, this fear of the unknown. What would I do without these amazing people in my life? Who would I be without this job that had become so much more than just a job?

But as the initial shock wore off, I realized this was an opportunity. A chance to step back, reassess, and maybe even chase some dreams of my own. And that's when the idea for Playful Acre took root.

So there I was, standing on the precipice of something new. I'd built a solid reputation in the childcare world and poured my heart and soul into creating a thriving in-home preschool. But a tiny voice inside kept whispering, "There's more." I was yearning to dive deeper into my passion for nature-based education, to expand beyond the confines of my living room and reach more families. But to do that, I knew I had to take a leap of faith, a grand jeté into the unpredictable world of entrepreneurship.

I channeled my inner marketing maven (honed from years of building my photography business) and got to work. Playful Acre, my very own nature-based preschool, was born. And within 30 days of that crazy idea taking root, I had a full class roster and a heart overflowing with gratitude.

For almost three years, I clung to this dream of being a full-time dreamer, doer, and businesswoman, all while rocking the homeschool mom gig. But eventually, reality hit. No one can do it all. We just can't. We need our village. And bringing in that village, just like I had for so many other moms, wasn't abandoning my dream of motherhood. It was expanding it. It showed my son what he would be capable of if he chased his own dreams. It was being the best mom I could possibly be by being the best *me* I could possibly be.

So, I made the tough decision to step away from childcare for the first time in over a decade. No safety net, just a burning desire to grow my media business and embrace the freelance life. I didn't know *exactly* how

I was going to replace a full-time income, but I trusted that by following my dreams—stepping into my creativity and business acumen and away from childcare—things would somehow work out.

And wouldn't you know it, the universe had my back. On the very last day of operating Playful Acre as a childcare business, just hours after I waved goodbye to my little crew, my phone rang. It was a colleague I'd been working with on a passion project—a little thing called Nanny Camp. It was this crazy dream I'd had, a whole elaborate plan I was about to pitch to her for sponsorship... only to have her approach me first, asking for help planning an almost identical event. Talk about serendipity!

That phone call wasn't just about Nanny Camp, though. This incredible woman, this leader, saw something in me that I hadn't yet discovered in myself. She saw my passion, my creativity, and my knack for connecting with people and building community. Instead of trying to fit me into a pre-defined box, she encouraged me to embrace those strengths, to bring my whole, messy, beautiful self to the table.

She raised me up and believed in me, not for what I could *do* for her, but for the unique magic I brought to the world. In doing so, she helped me to find my dream. It takes a village to raise a child, but it also takes a villa to raise a mother. And it takes a village to raise a dream.

A dream that's still unfolding, a tapestry woven with vibrant threads of storytelling, connection, and boundless creativity. It's a dream that takes me around the world, connecting with incredible people, exploring new cultures, and showing my son the vastness of what's possible. It's a dream that pushes me to optimize, to innovate, to lead, and to inspire—within our company, our industry, and my own family.

It's a dream that has opened doors I never knew existed, doors that lead to greatness, not just for me but for everyone who dares to step through them. And it all started with a leap of faith, a whispered "yes" to the unknown.

These days, I'm the marketing director at Adventure Nannies and spend my days educating and empowering nannies, educators, and families on how to find pathways toward crafting lives that honor their unique passions and dreams. I am transforming the Playful Acre brand from a nature-based daycare to immersive retreats to help adults embrace the creativity and joy that come from experiential learning in the great outdoors, all while keeping my photography business on the side to continue to uplift families by capturing the fleeting moments of their kids' lives, both epic and every day. And I'm a present, loving, and adventurous parent to my amazing son.

As I sit here and reflect on my journey over the past seven years as a mom, going from "just a nanny" to "just a mom" to a woman who dared to follow her heart, I see how those whispers of doubt have transformed into a roar of possibility. I've conquered my own insecurities about motherhood thanks to the powerful women, many of them moms themselves, who have encouraged and mentored me through the simple act of being their authentic selves. It was proof that I was capable of **more**. It wasn't about being *better* than being a mom, but about being a mom *and* **more**. A mom who chases her dreams embraces adventure and shows her son that the world is his for the taking. And that, my friends, is what motherhood is truly about.

About Reagan Fulton

Reagan Fulton is a passionate advocate for play, a champion for nannies, and a creative force in the childcare industry. As the Marketing Director for Adventure Nannies and co-creator of Nanny Camp, she empowers caregivers to connect with nature, rediscover the joy of play, and find deeper purpose in their work.

Her journey has been a tapestry woven with creativity, adventure, and a deep love for the natural world. From her early days as a nanny to her current leadership role, she's consistently sought ways to inspire and uplift those around her through her storytelling and art.

Reagan is a firm believer in the power of serendipity, the magic of everyday moments, and the importance of chasing your dreams with a playful heart.

Conclusion

By Shenandoah Davis

If you are a nanny or aspiring nanny who has followed the hero's tales scattered throughout this book, I hope you've found a piece of every story you can identify with or aspire to. Please remember that your story deserves to be told too—to us, to other nannies, to future employers, and to your families. We know how vulnerable and isolating working in someone else's home can be, and we have also seen how a few sparks of community can create bonfires of connection.

To all of those we've already had the privilege of meeting and working with, thank you for being part of our story and allowing us to learn from you over the years. We hope you share our pride in what we've created together.

The interesting thing about each of the nannies who contributed to this book is that most of their stories would never fit into a standard resume. So often, we see families focusing on a few surface-level details when thinking about who they will hire as a nanny instead of being brave enough to take a deeper dive and invest some time into getting to know the person they'll be trusting to spend forty or more hours a week in their home with their beloved kids. While the ten folks featured in this book are truly incredible, they have also been rejected by families with a quick glance at their profile—for not having a Bachelor's degree, for not having enough years of experience with a certain age group, for not speaking a certain language that neither parent speaks either. One thing I have learned after meeting thousands of families and nannies over the past ten-plus years is that everyone has their own story and their own superpowers they bring to the table, and when you open yourself up to learning, you may end up with the nanny you needed the most, not the one you imagined.

We can't sit down with a pen and paper and design the human we want to marry, raise, or hire. Our company is not perfect because we are human-centered and human-powered, and humans are perfectly imperfect in their own ways. The next time you are thinking about who to bring into your household and who to trust as part of your family's village, we hope you will reflect on some of the incredible humans in this book and open your horizons to someone who may not check every box but will create some new boxes you weren't even aware of and bring new horizons, enrichment, and of course, adventure to your family's lives.

Made in the USA
Middletown, DE
31 March 2025